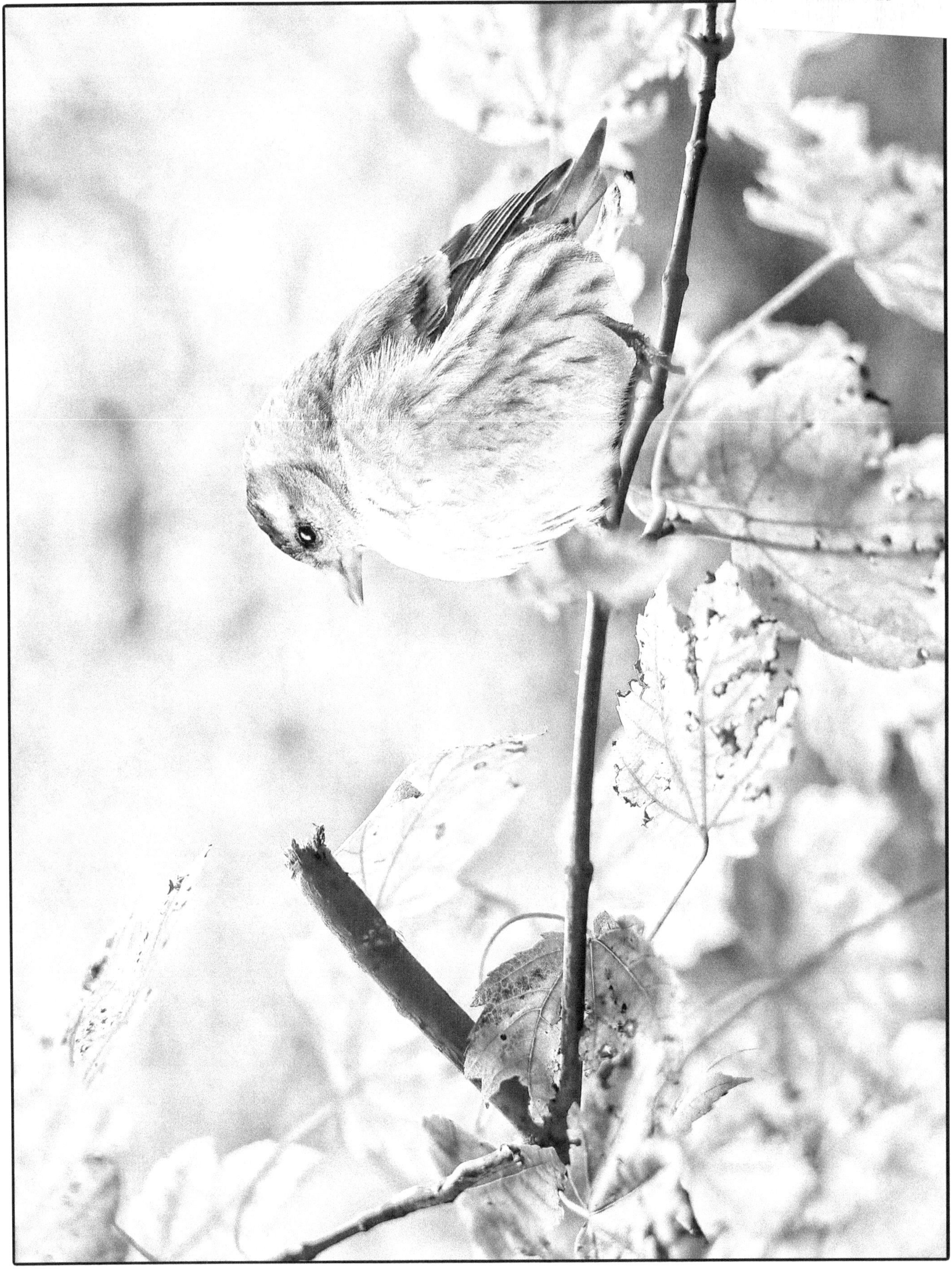

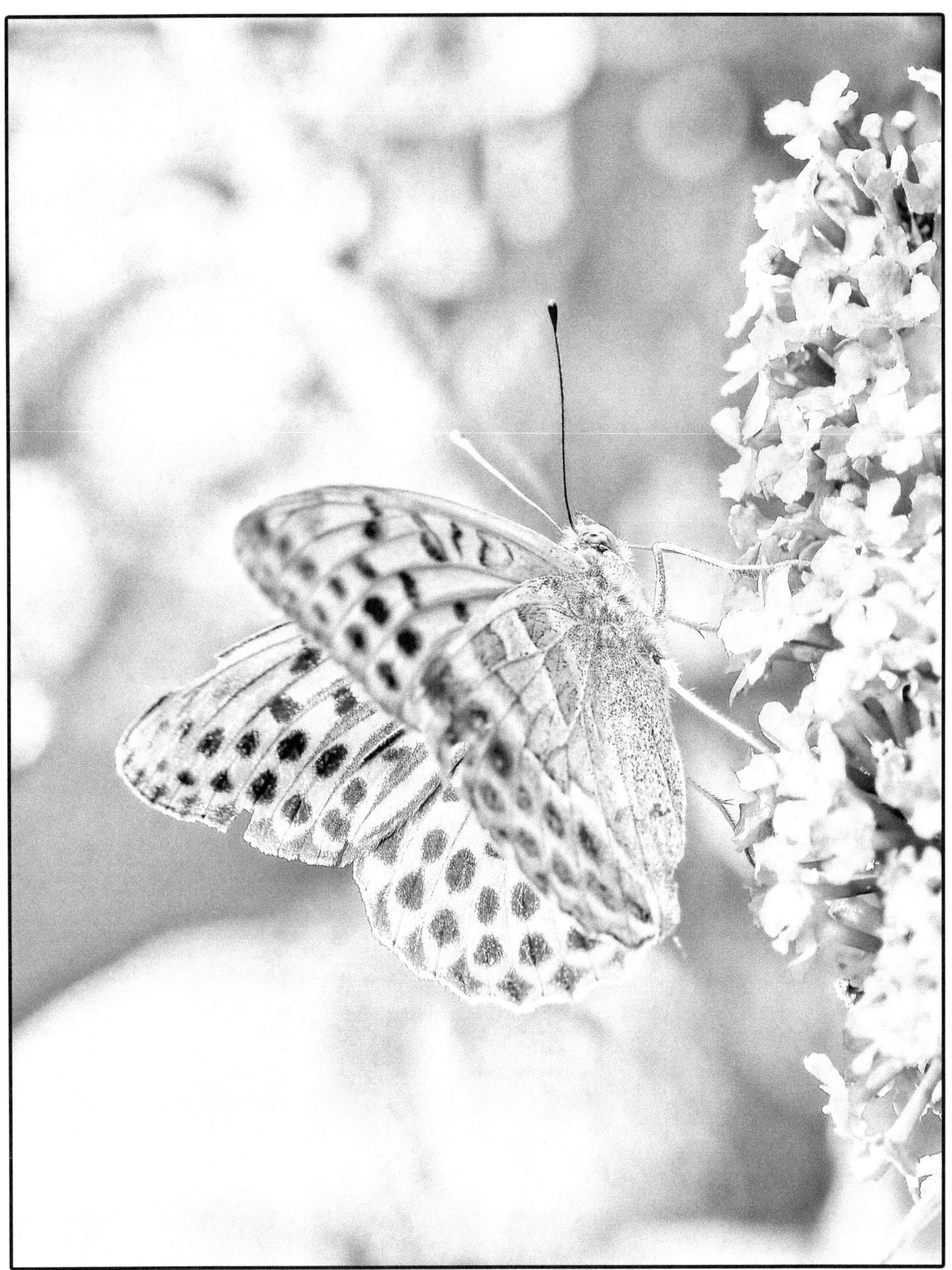

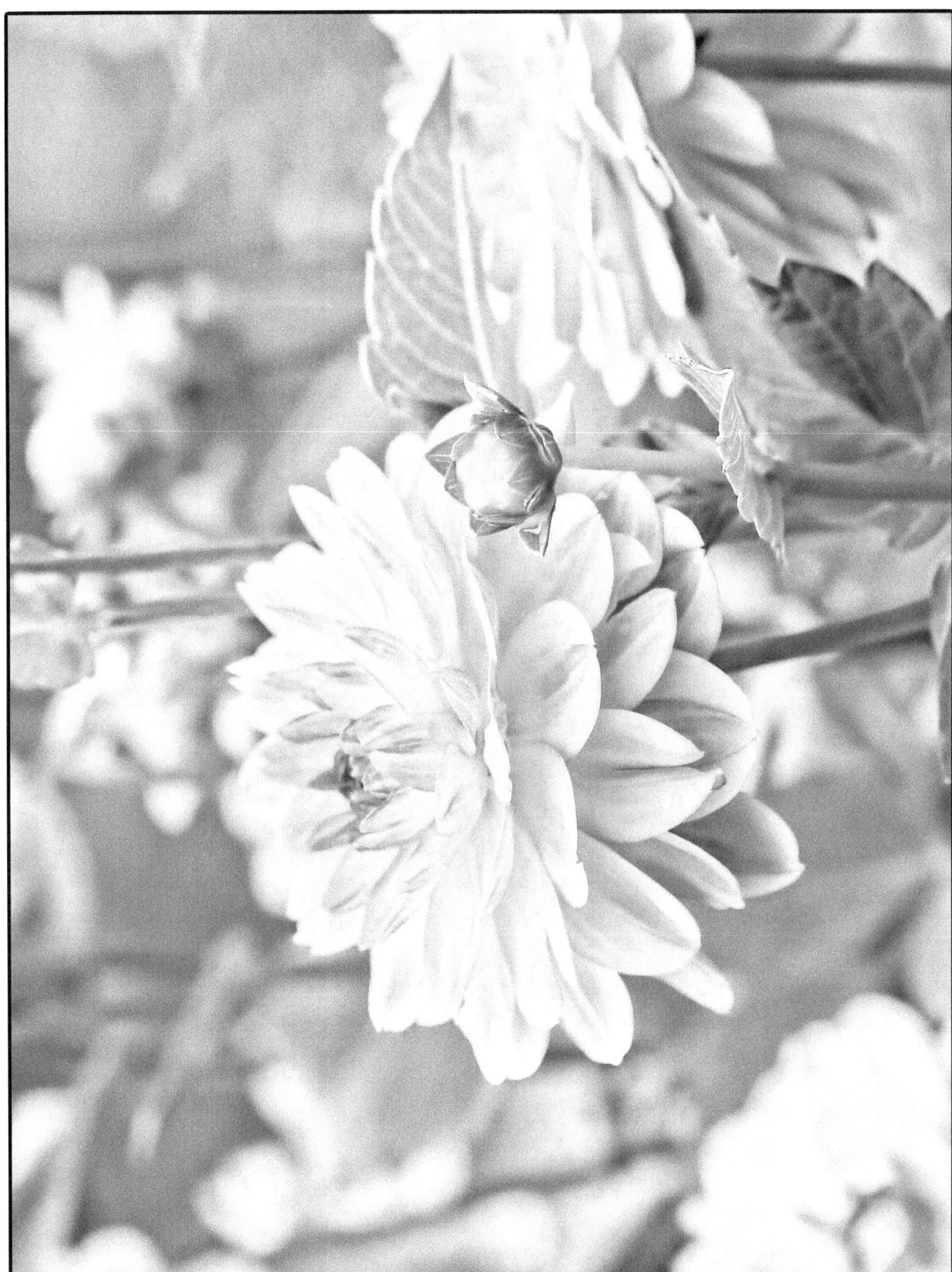

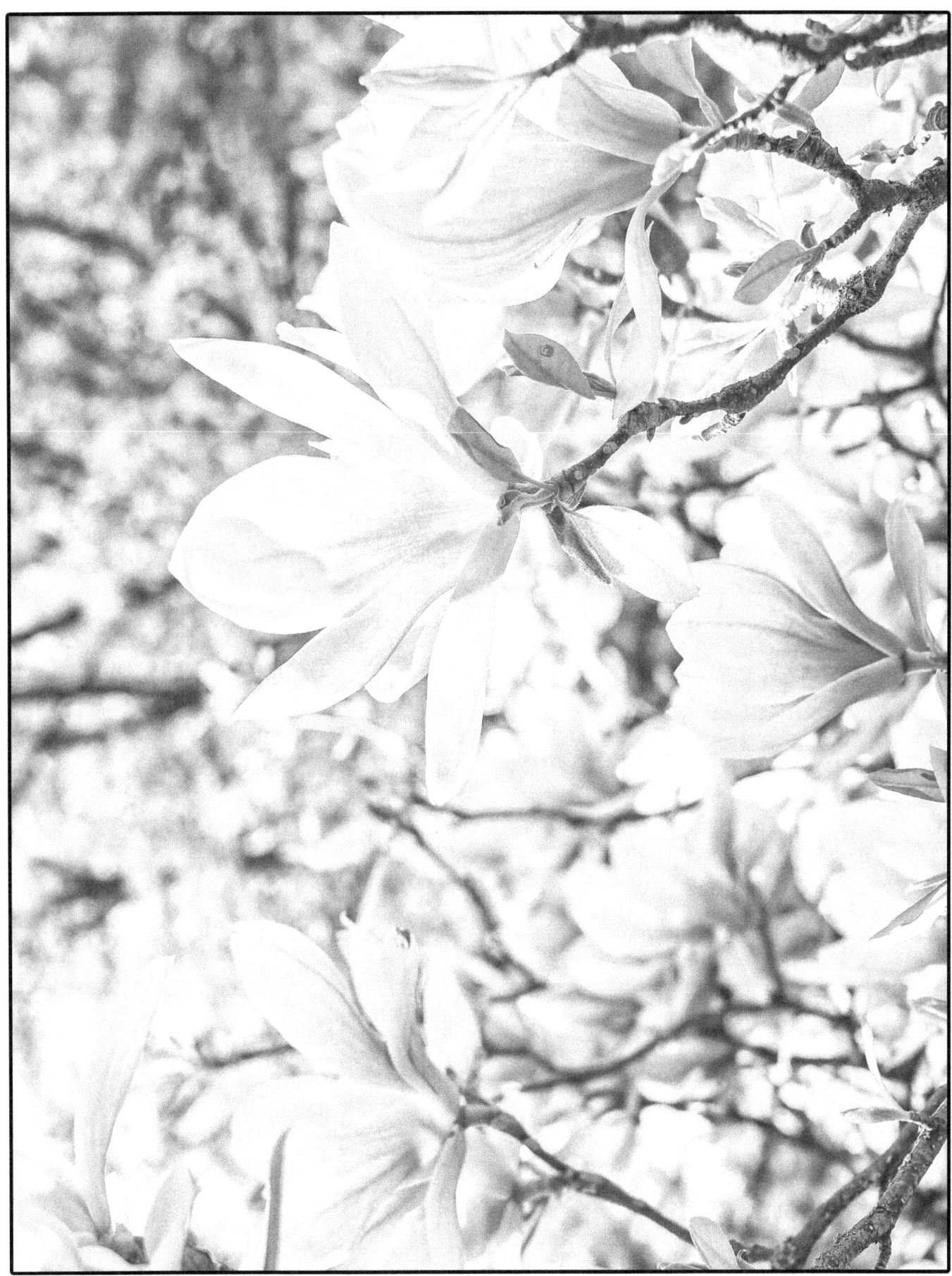

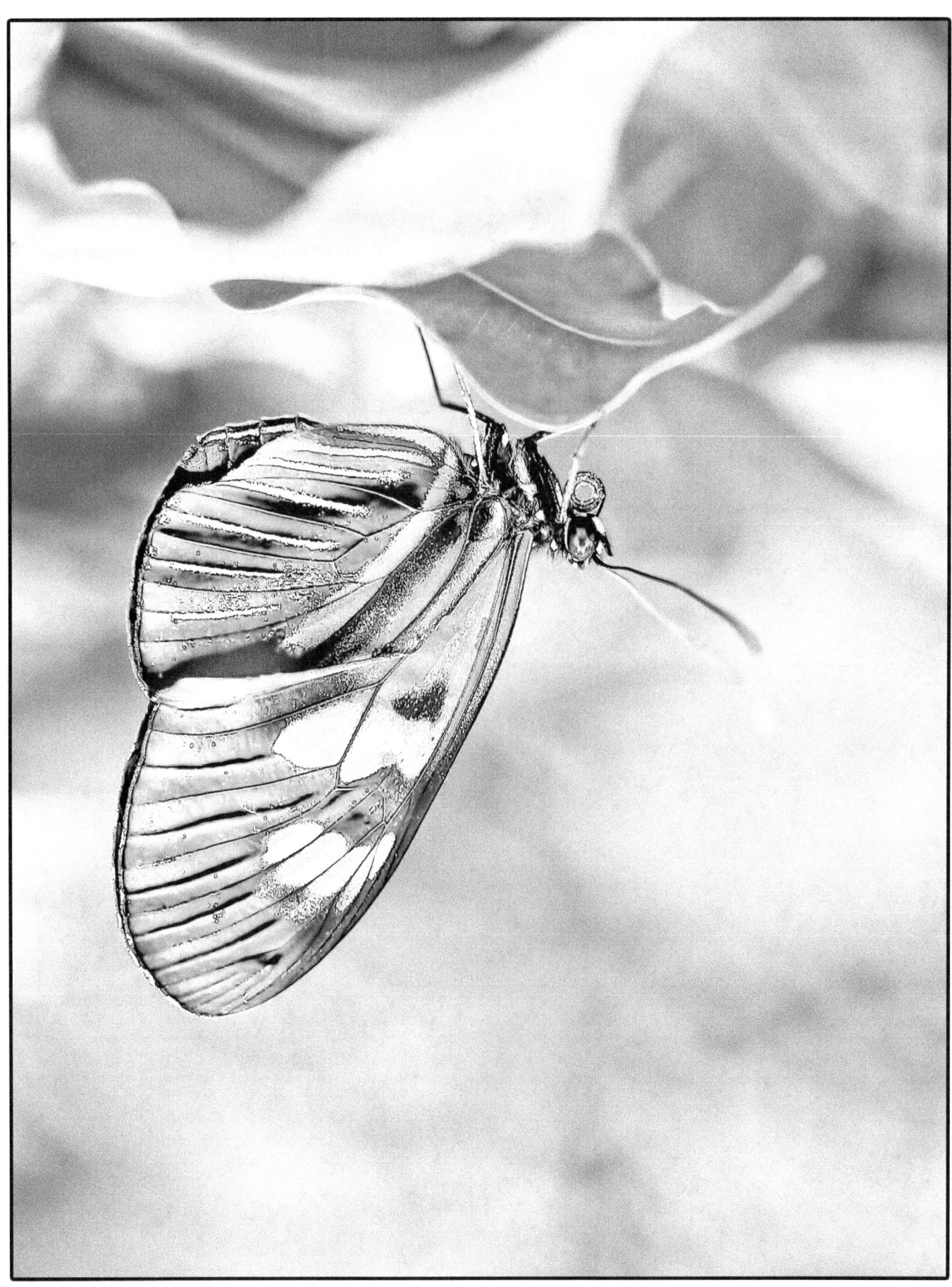

Try to color something else...

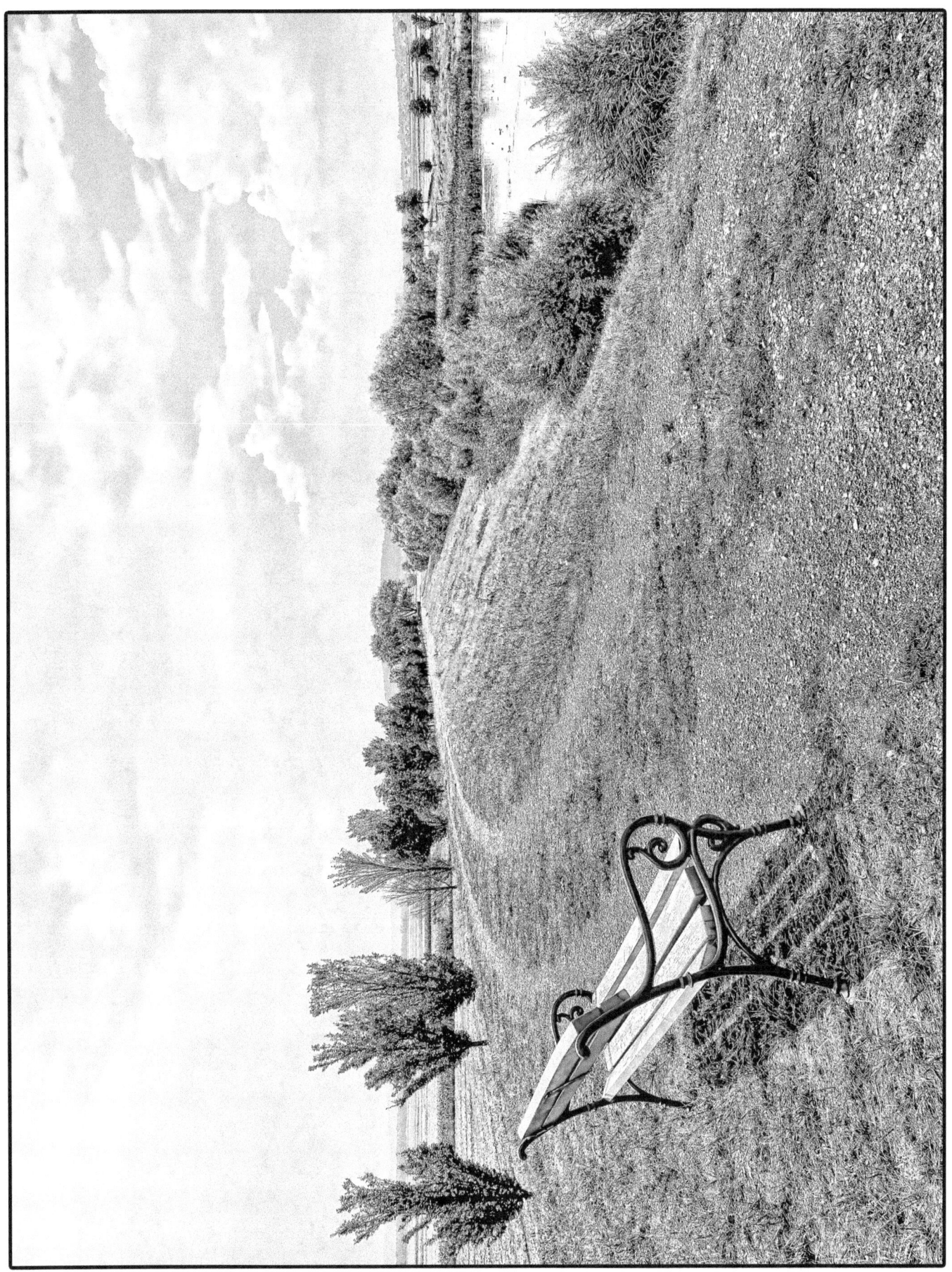

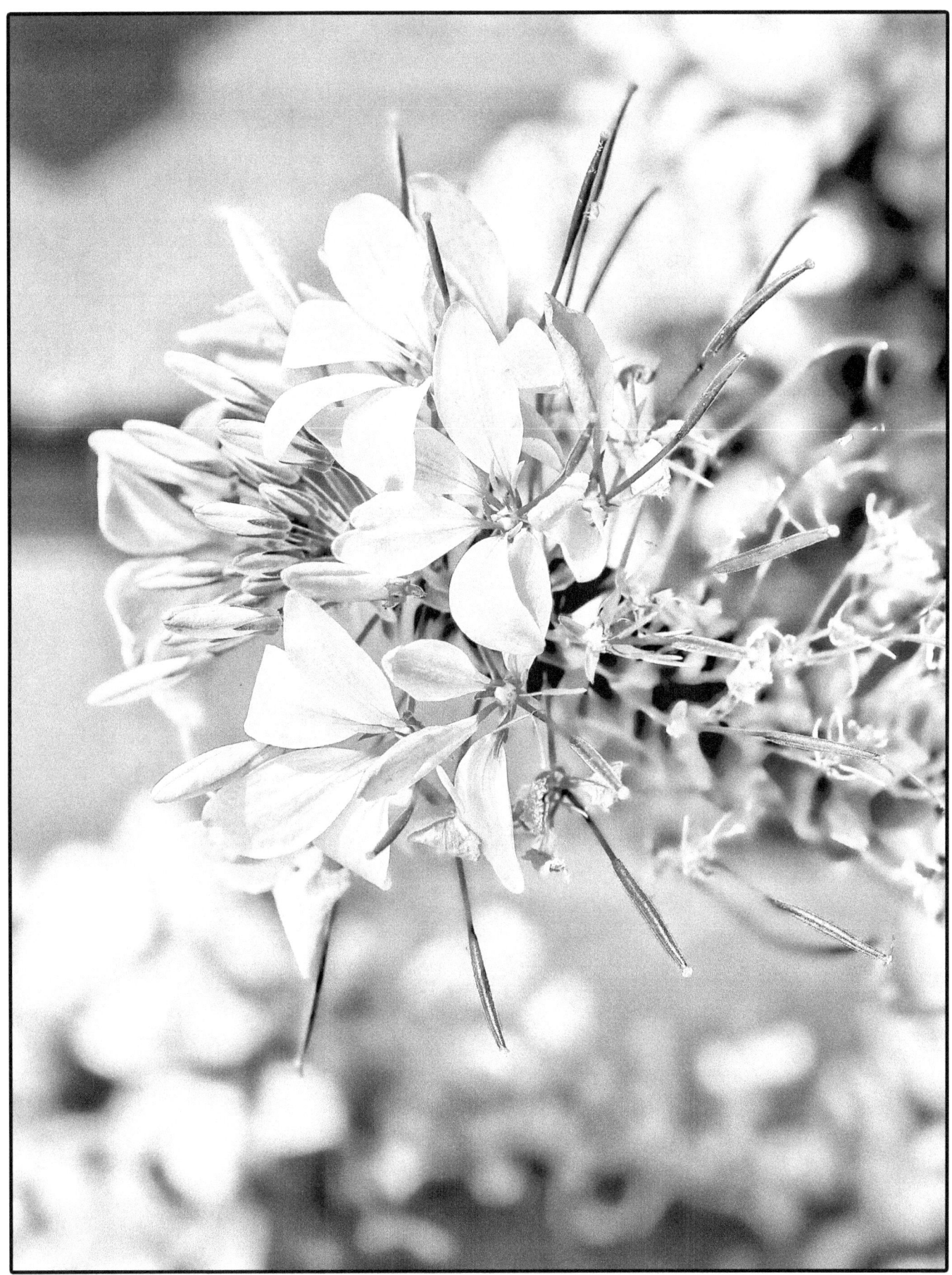

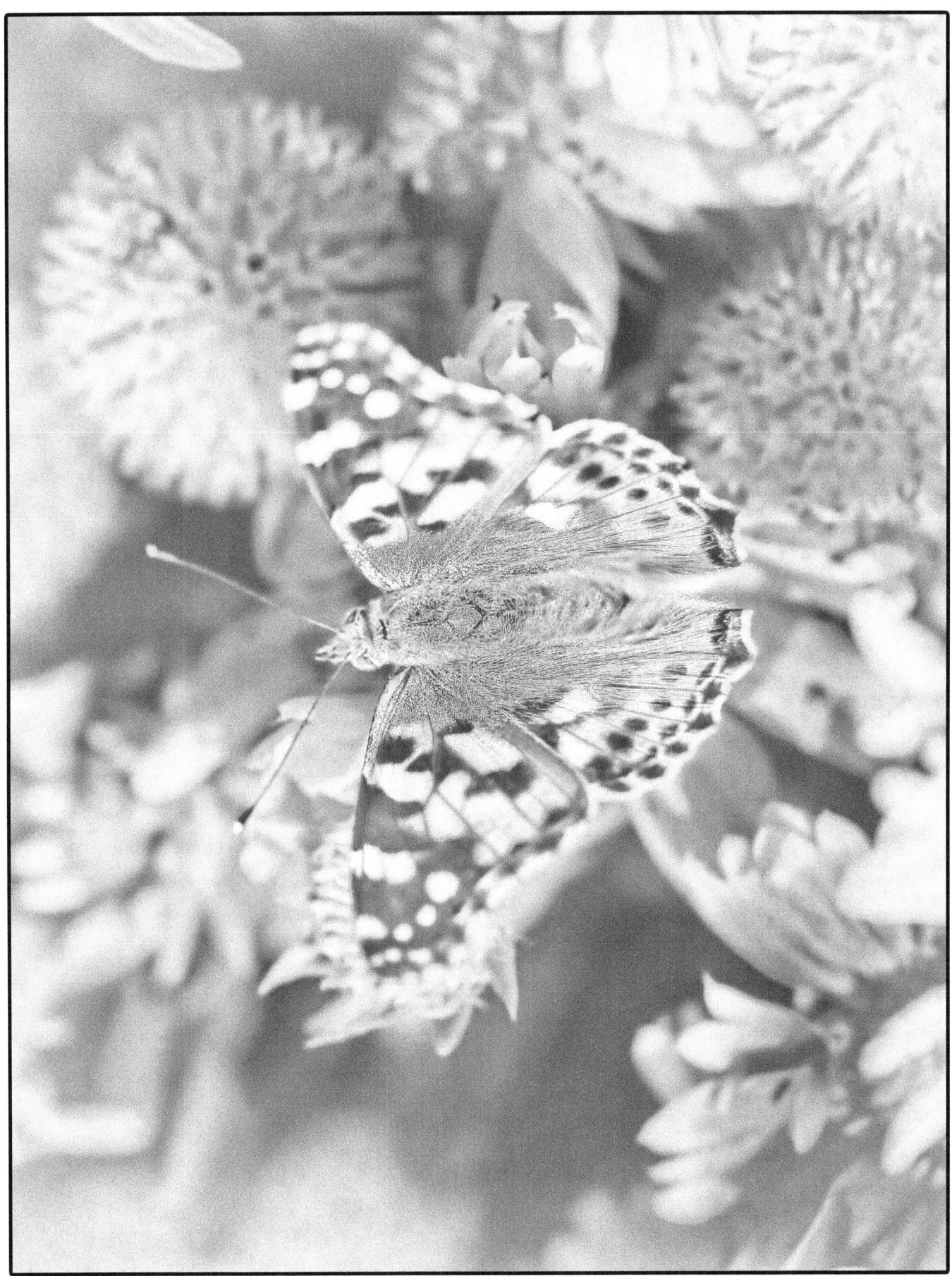

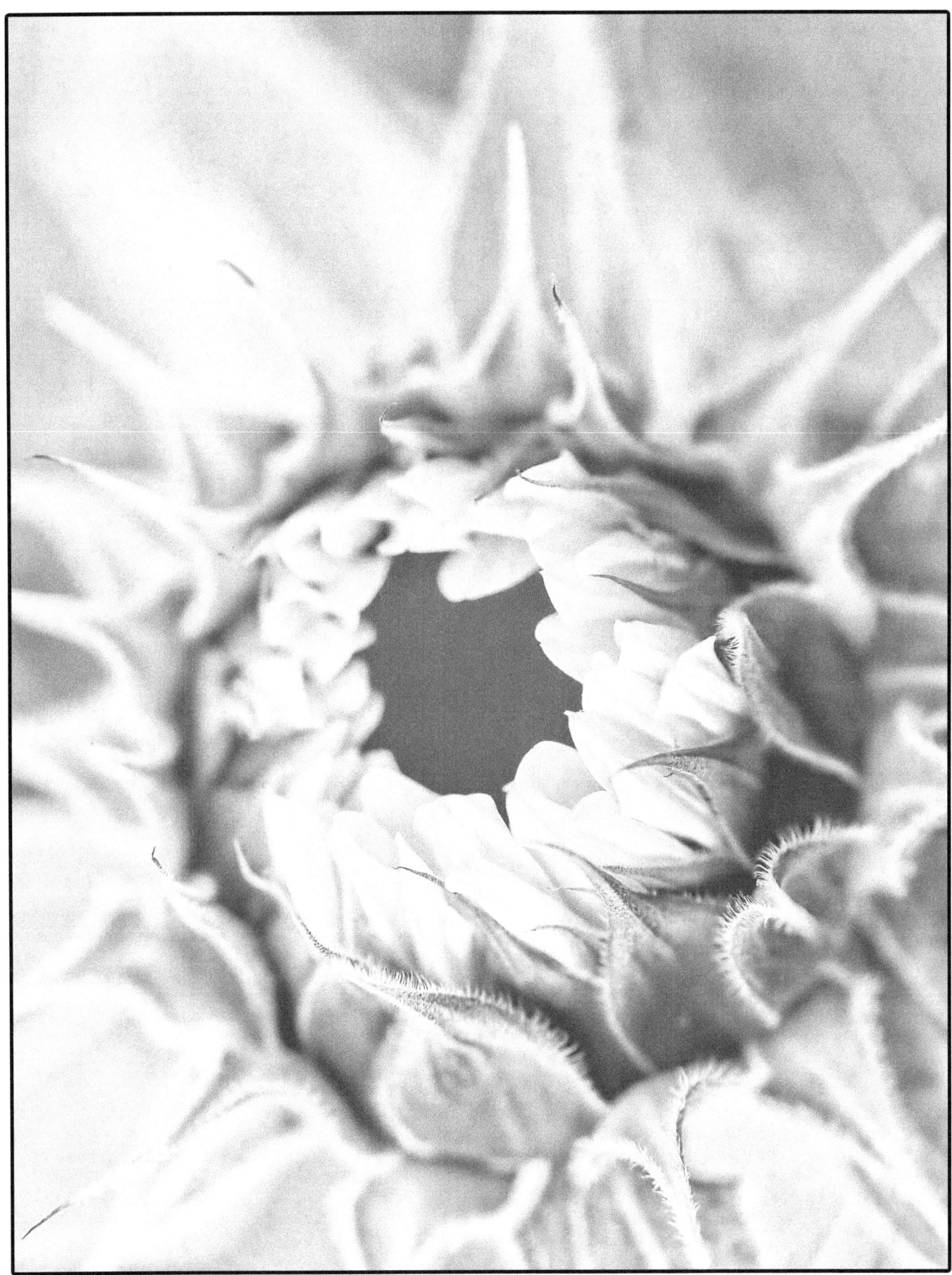

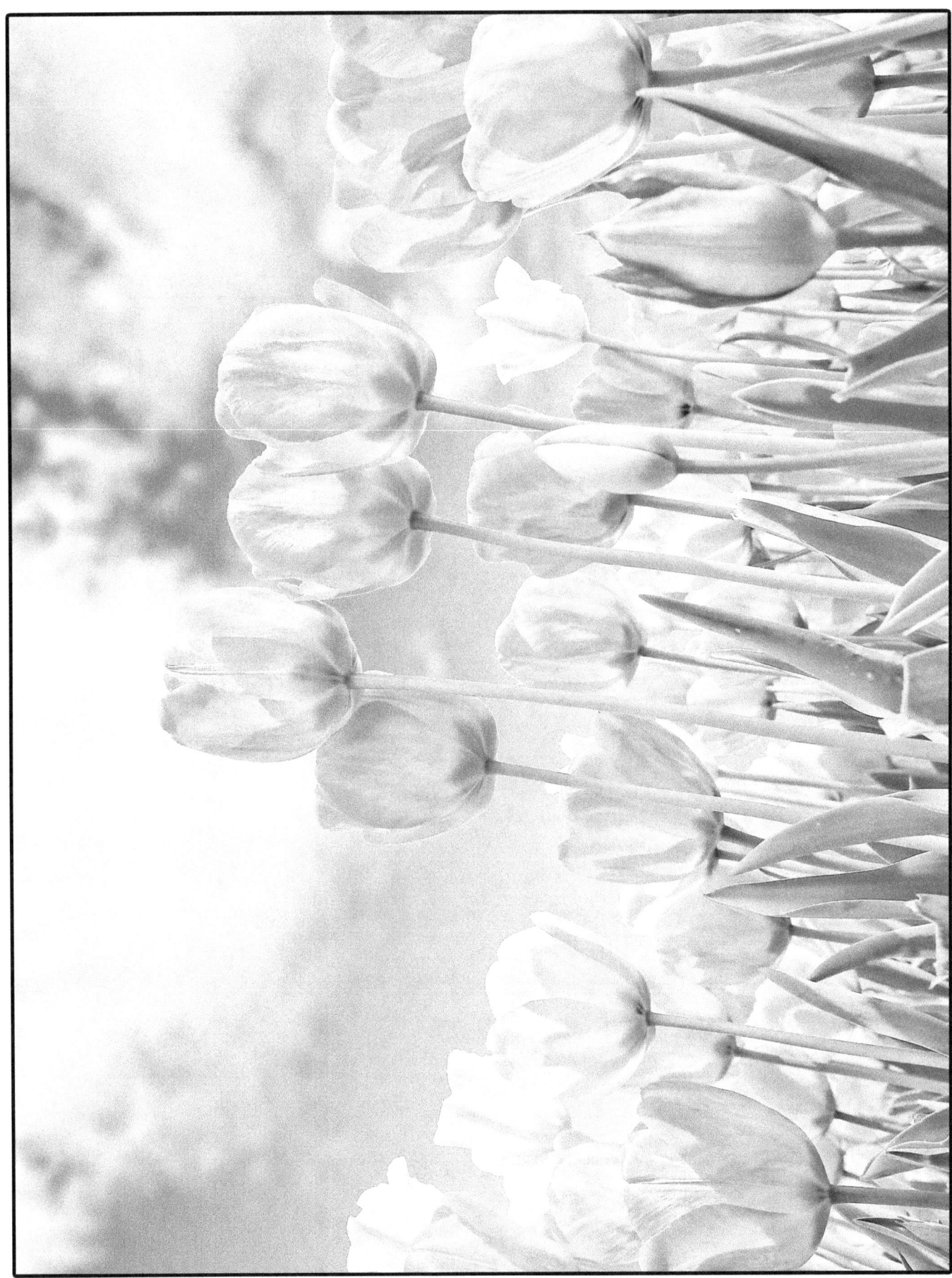

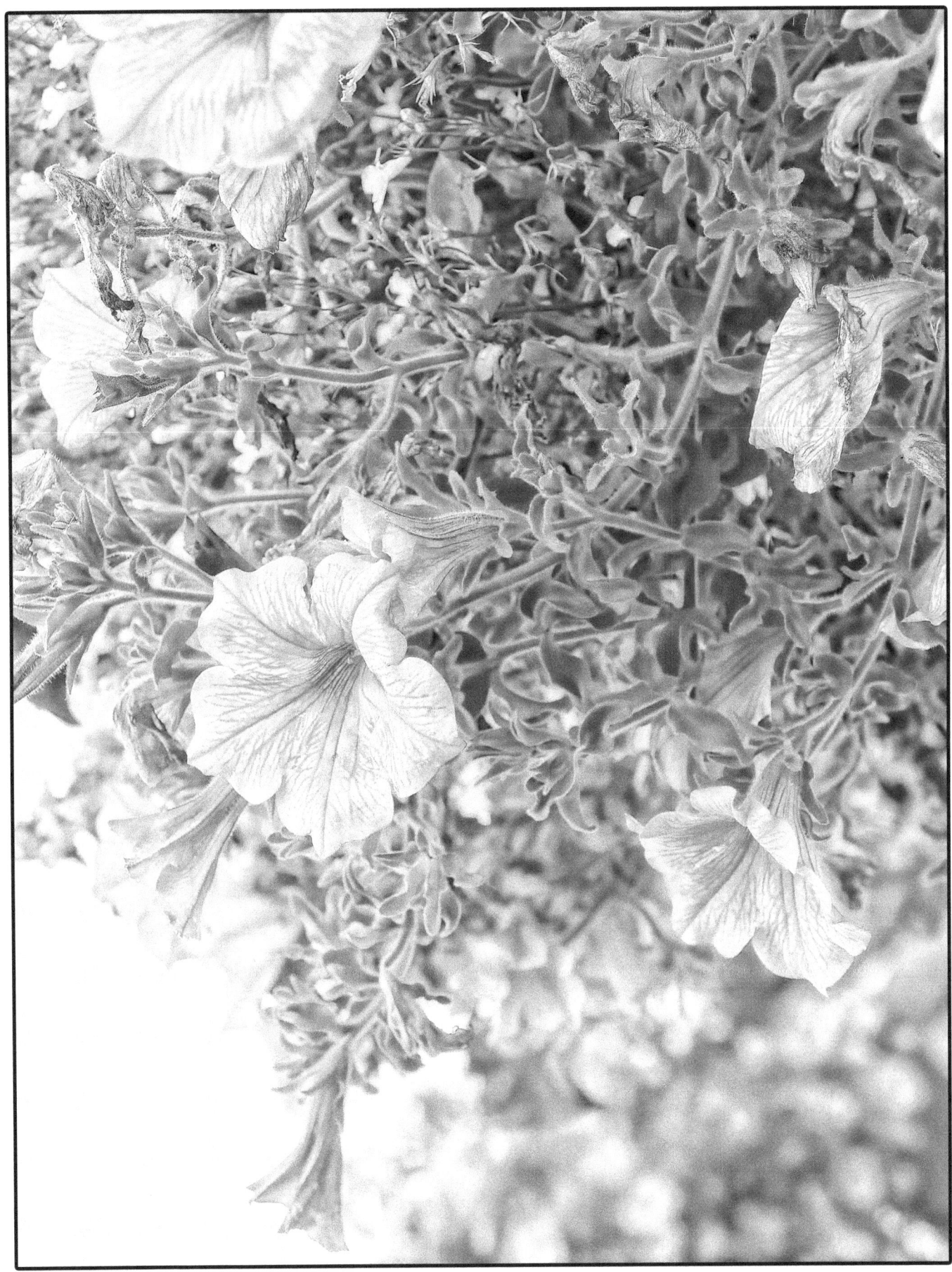

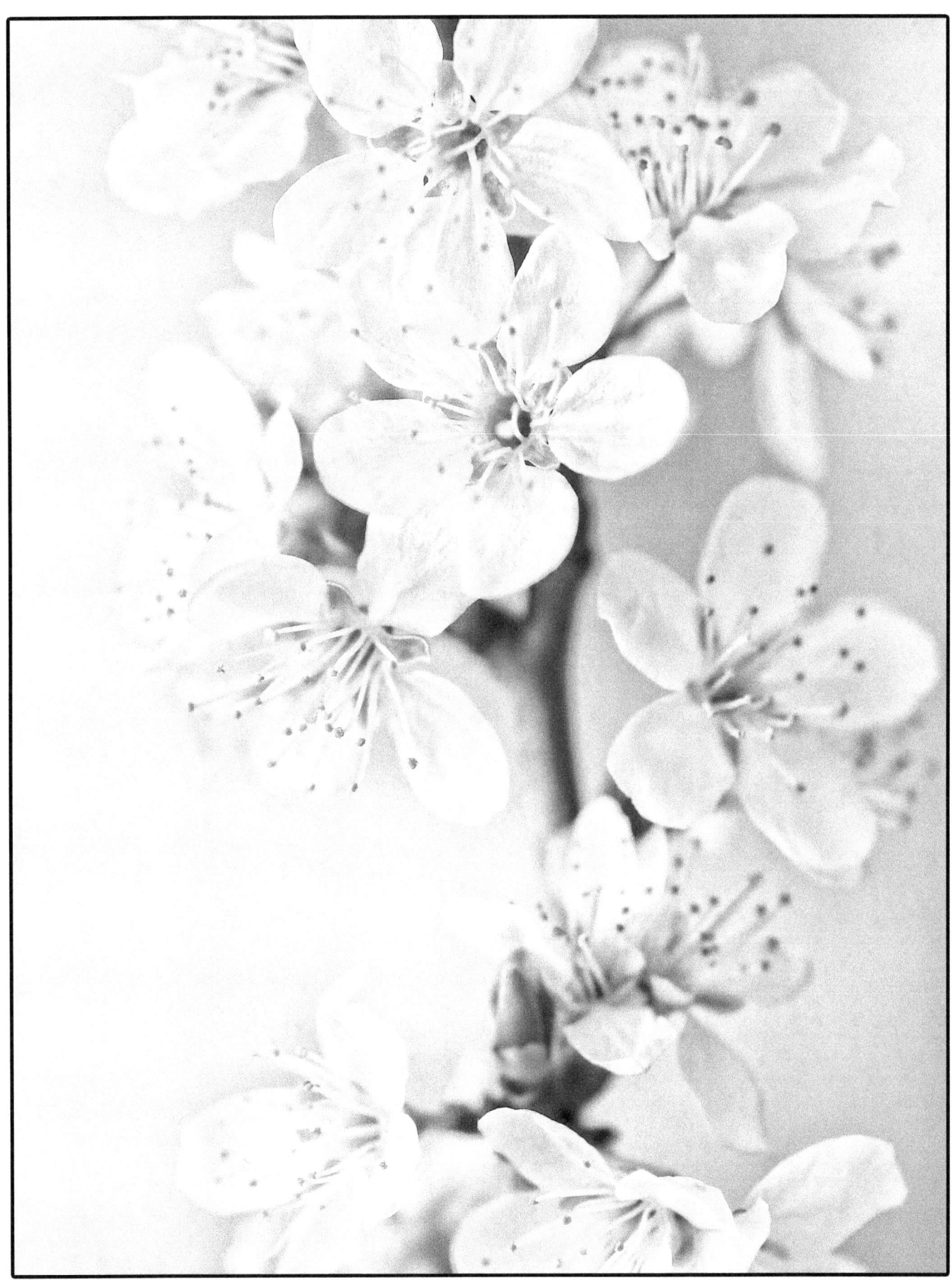

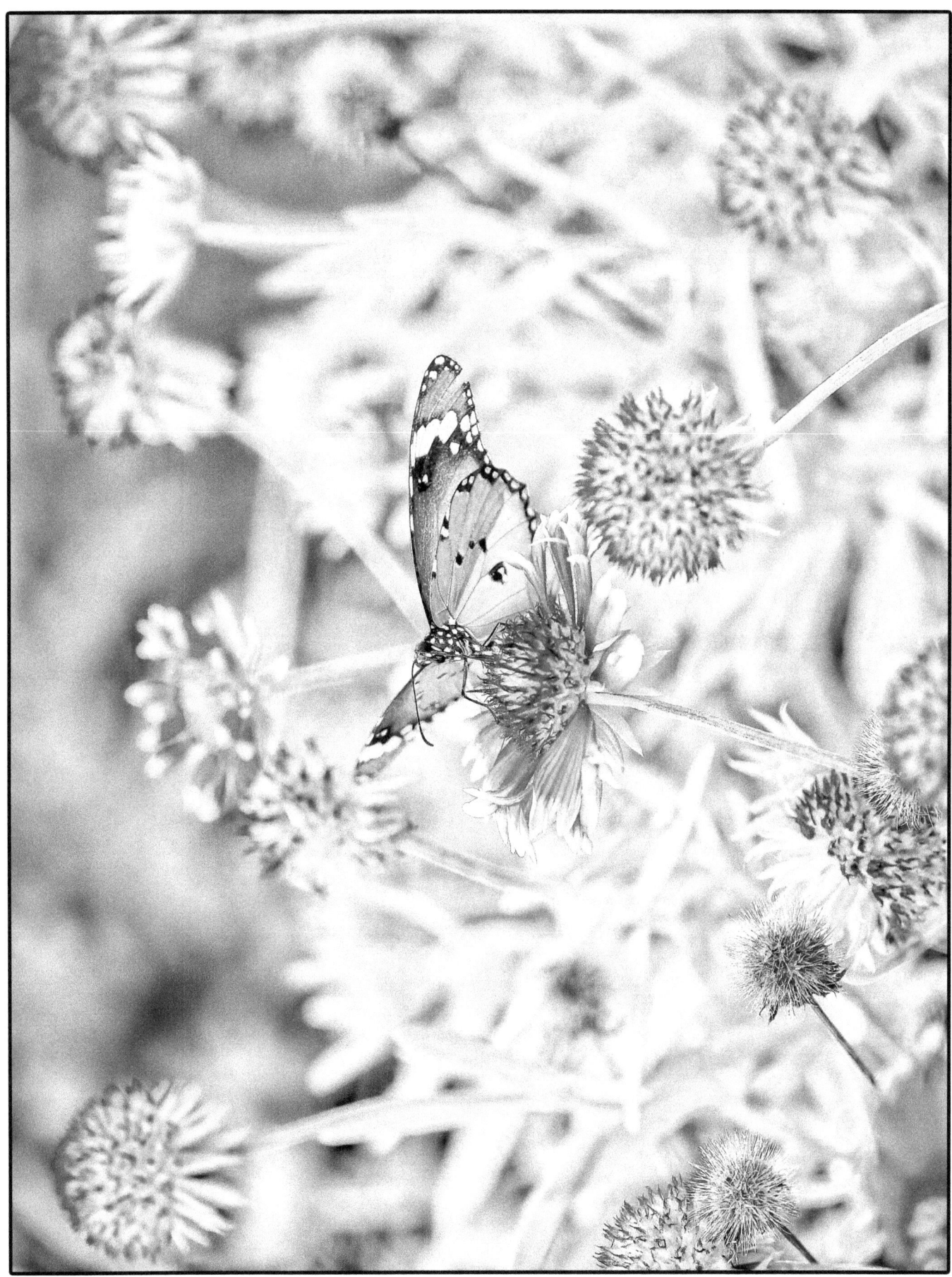

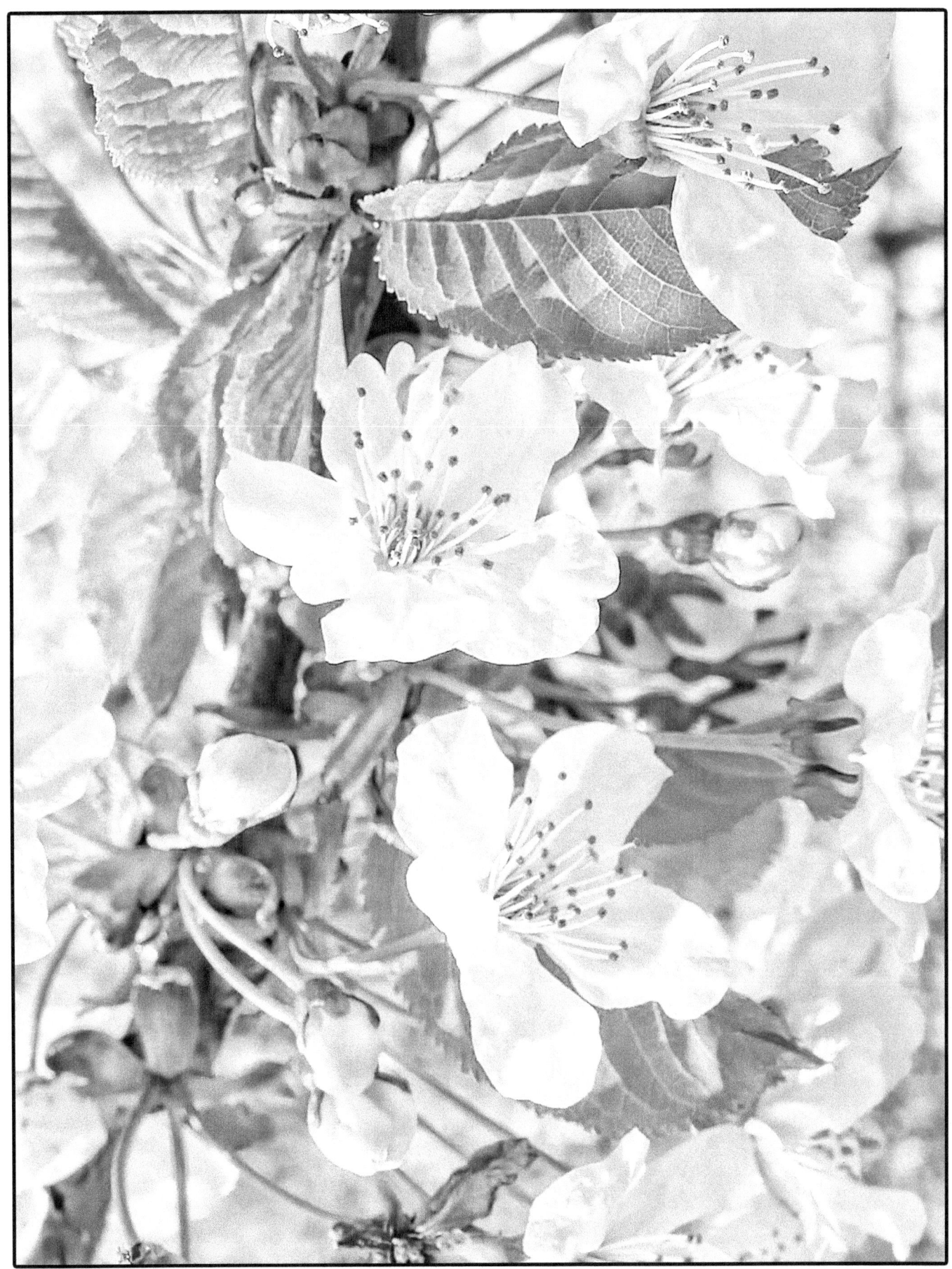

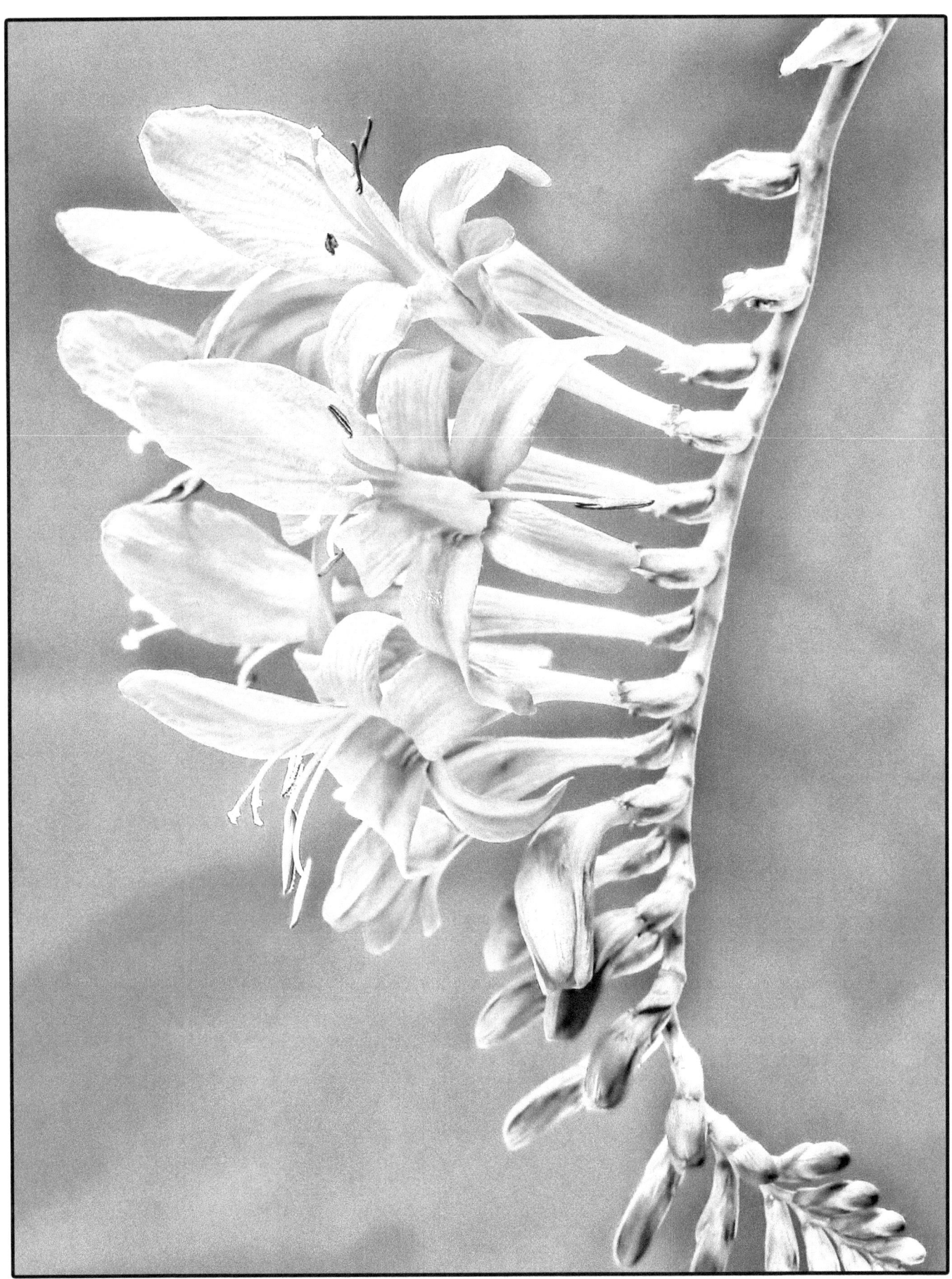

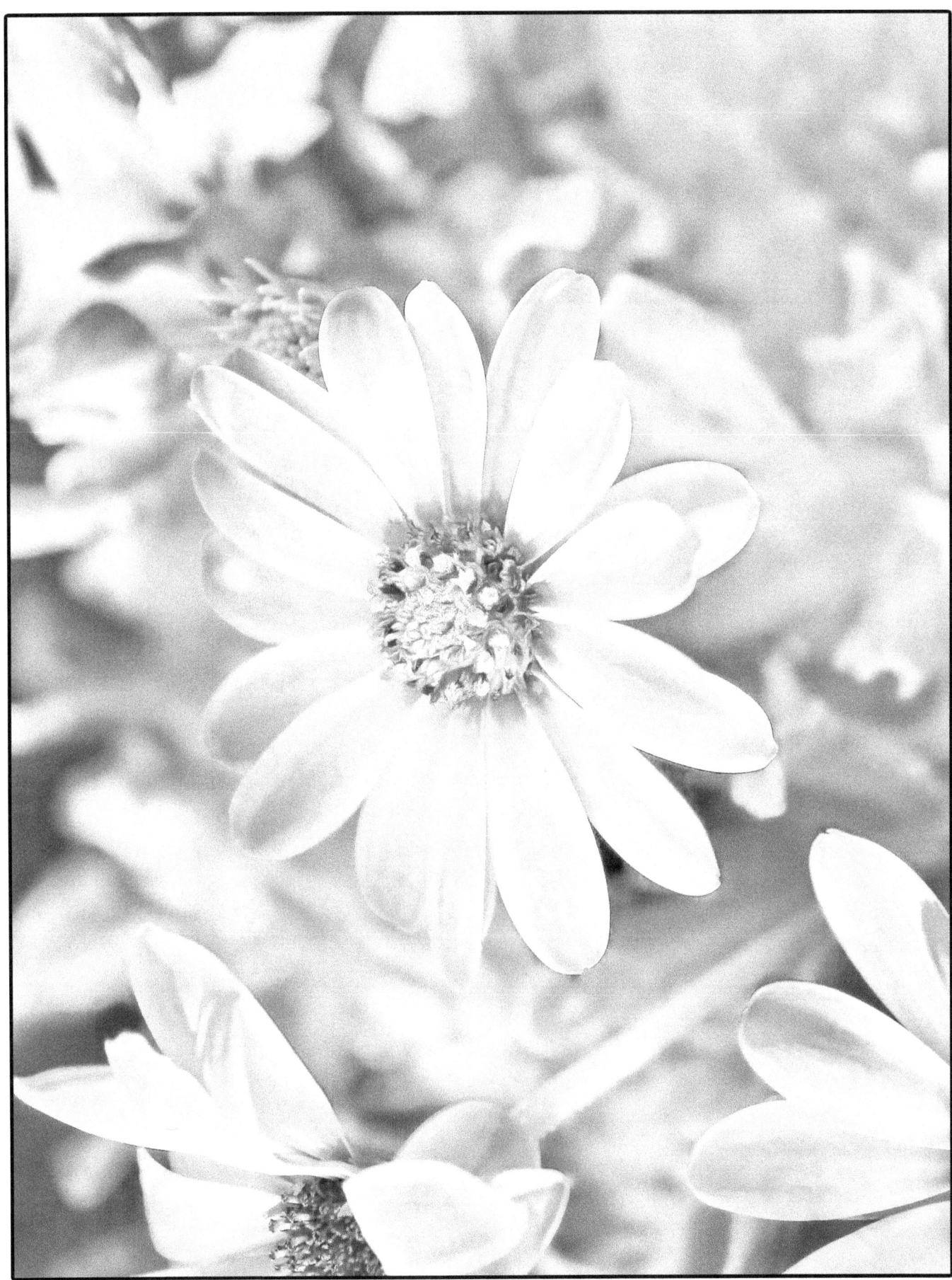

Try to color something else...

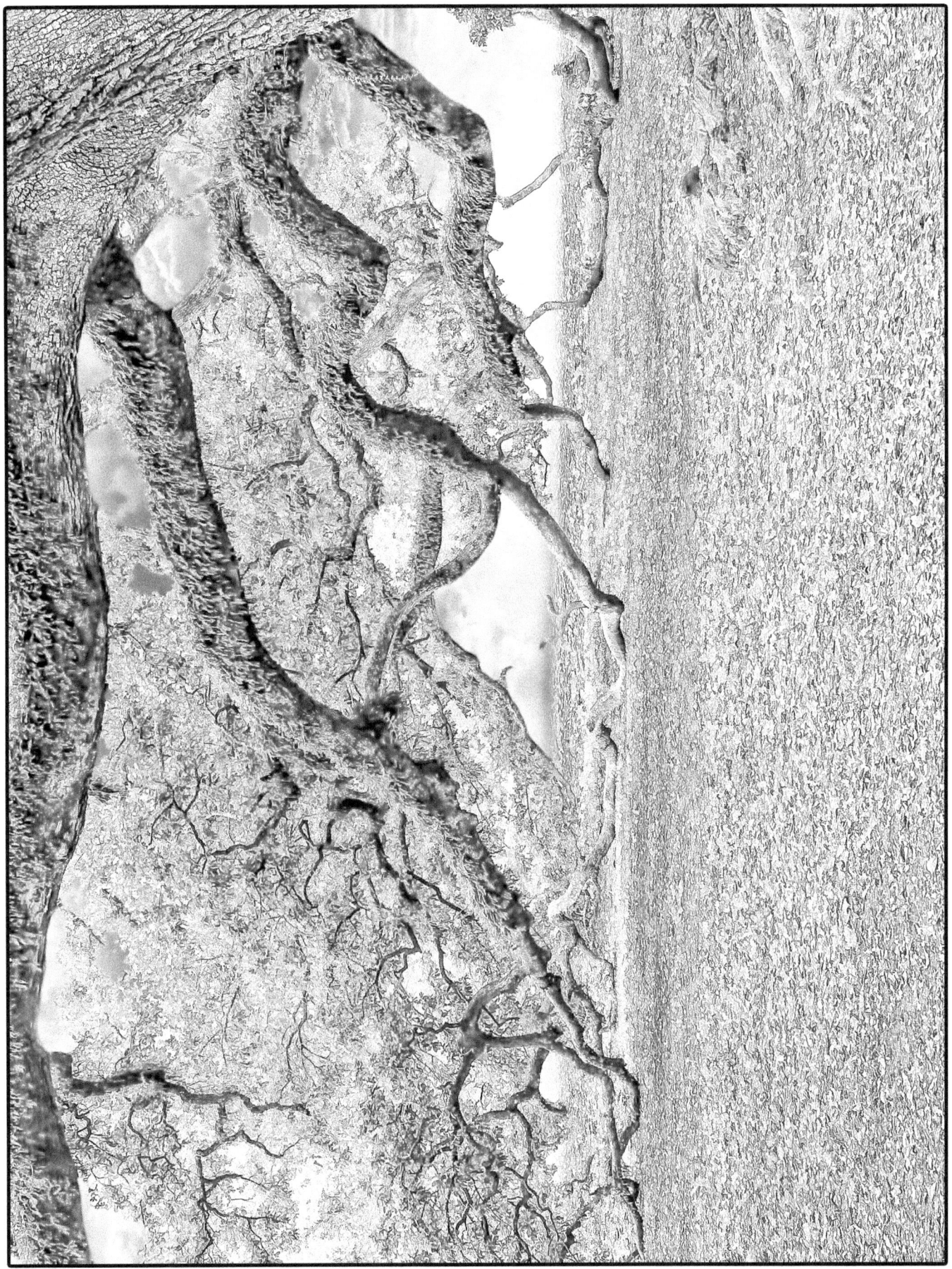

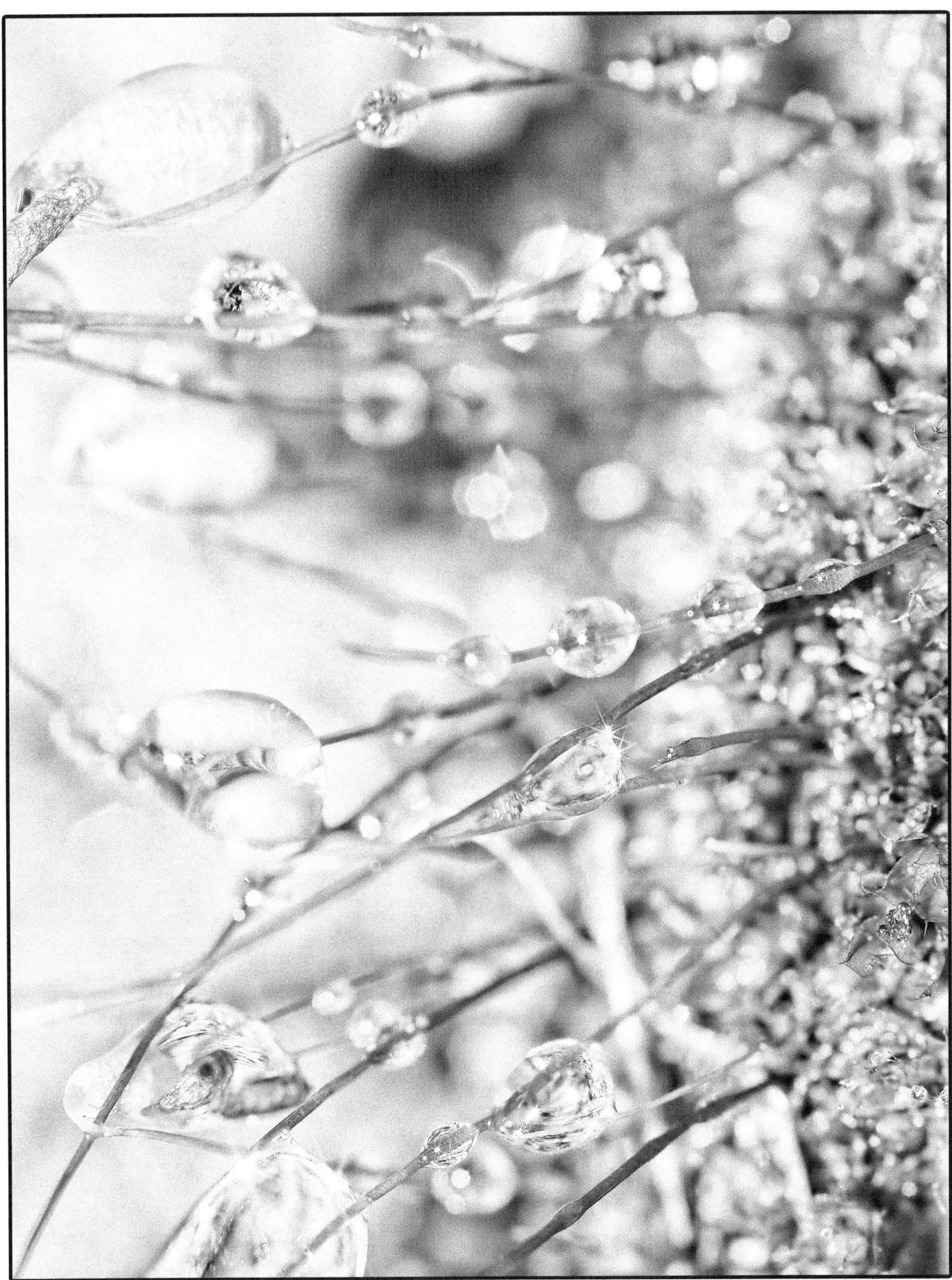

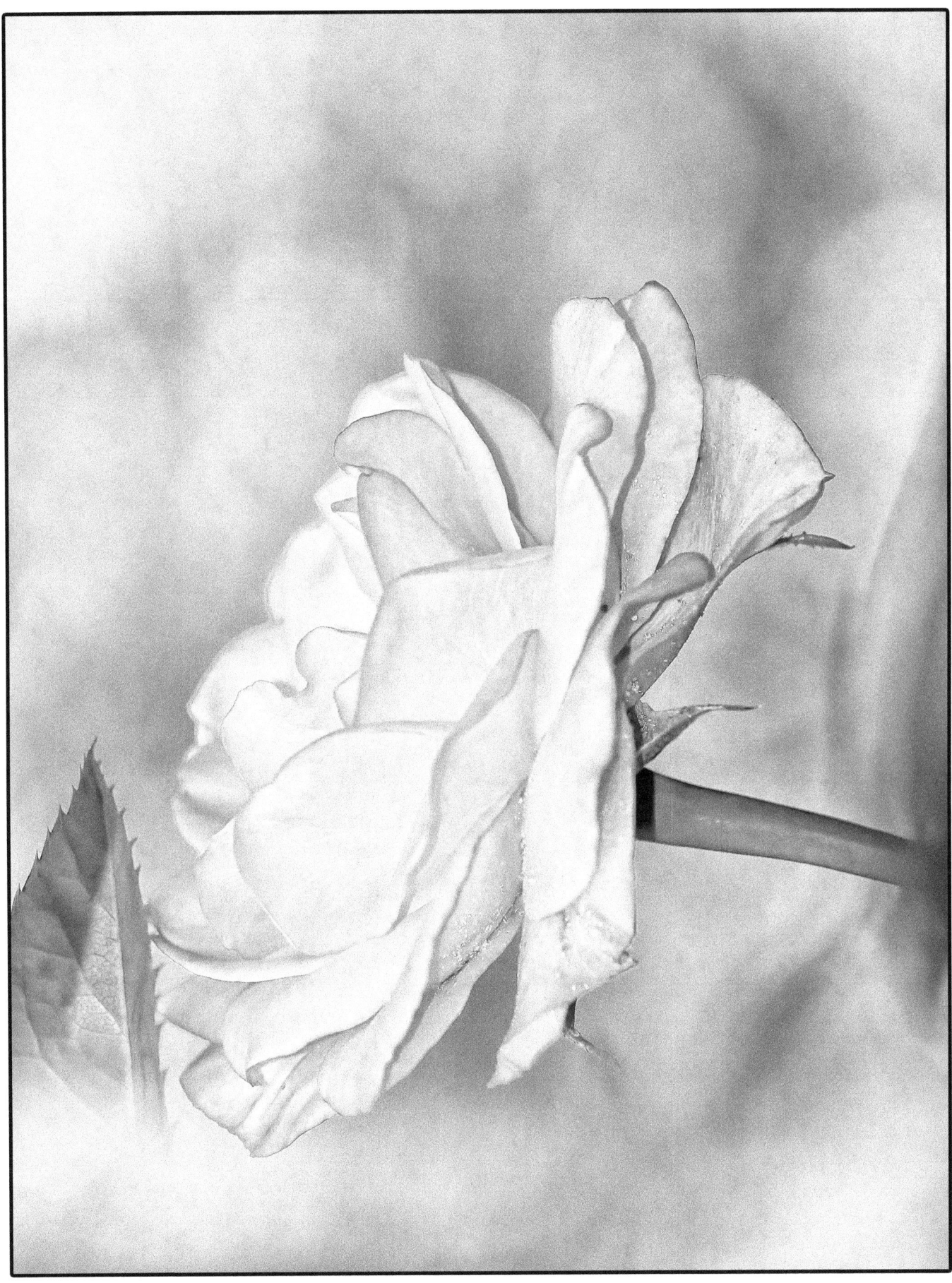

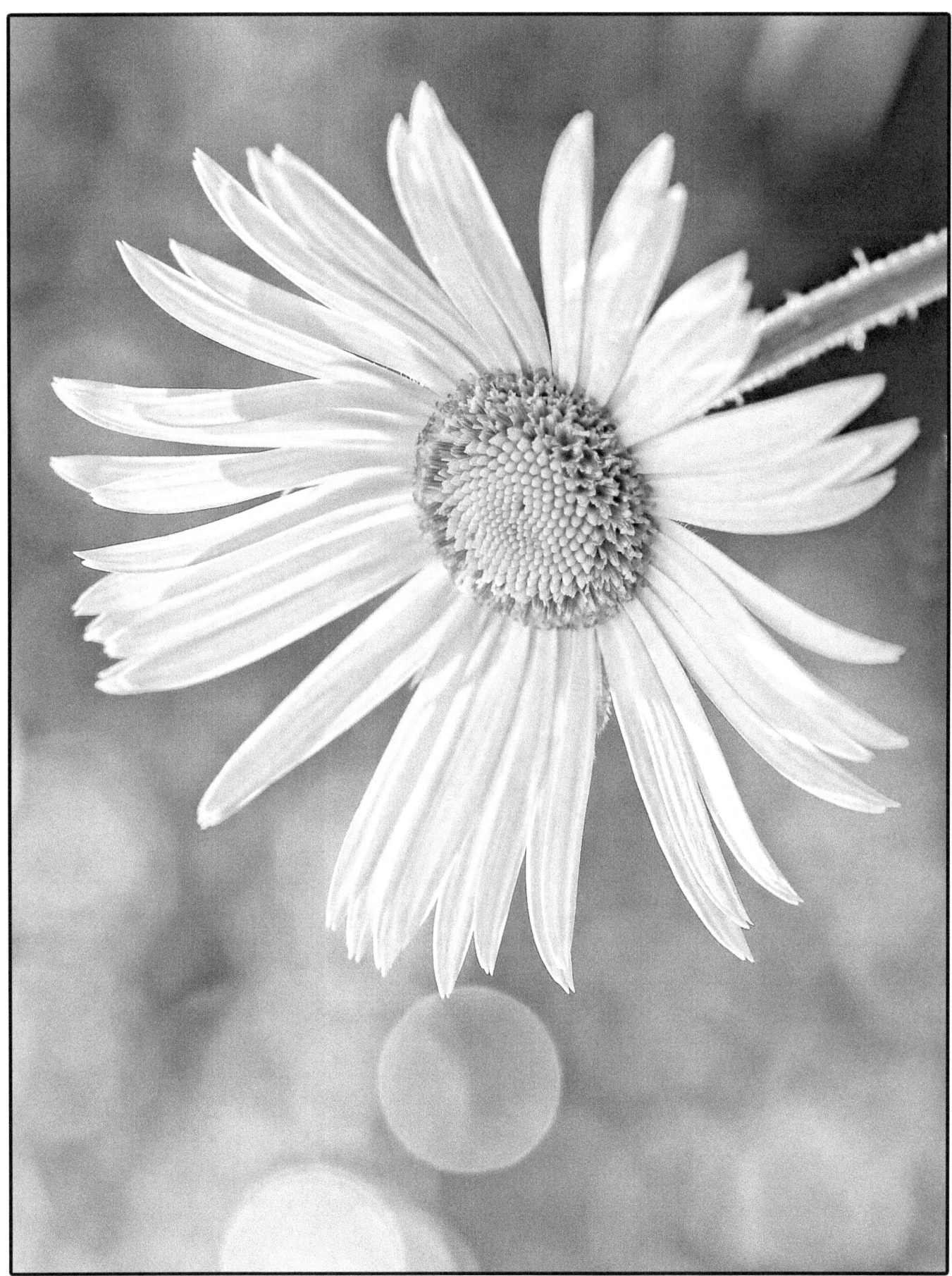

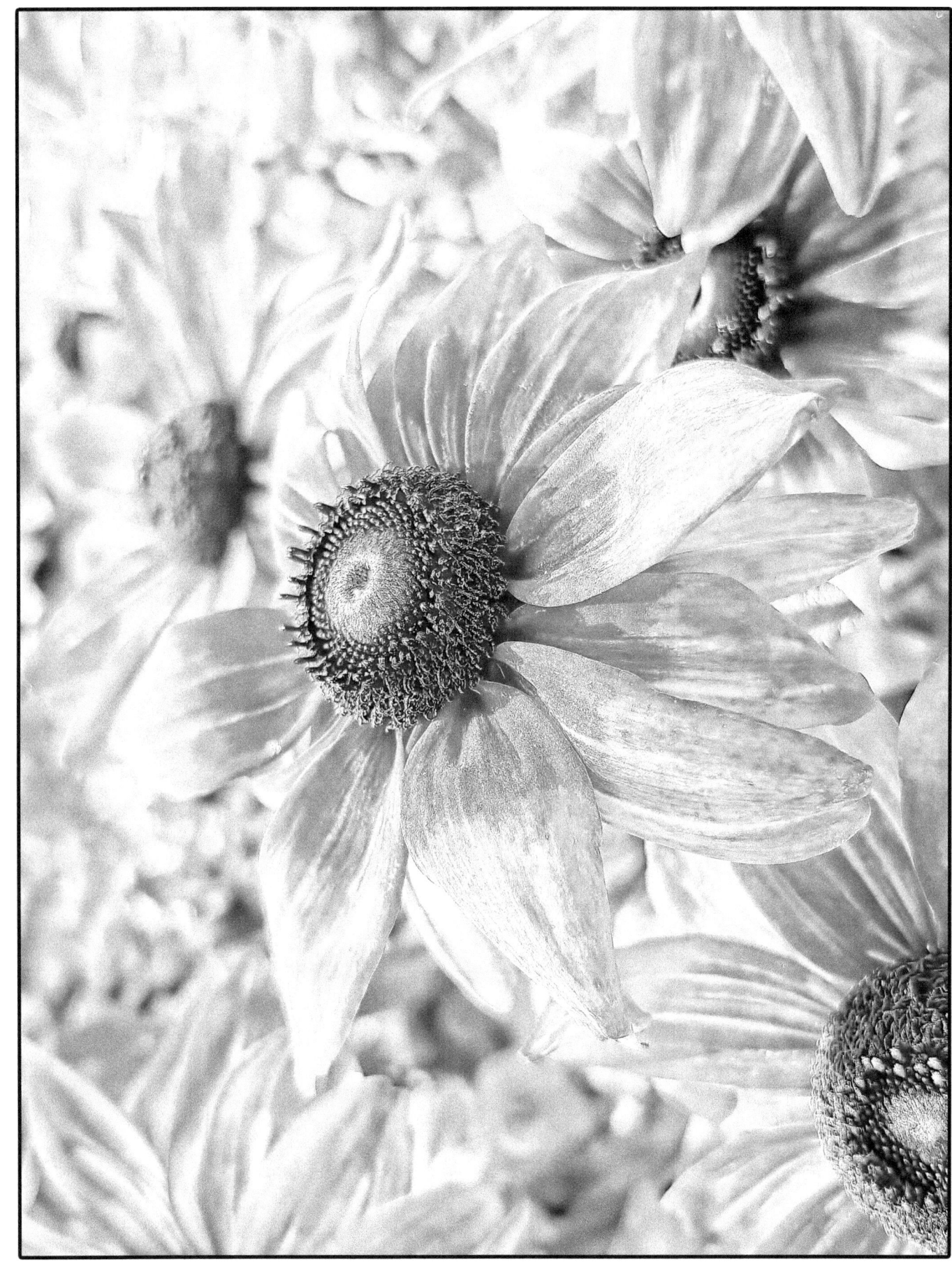

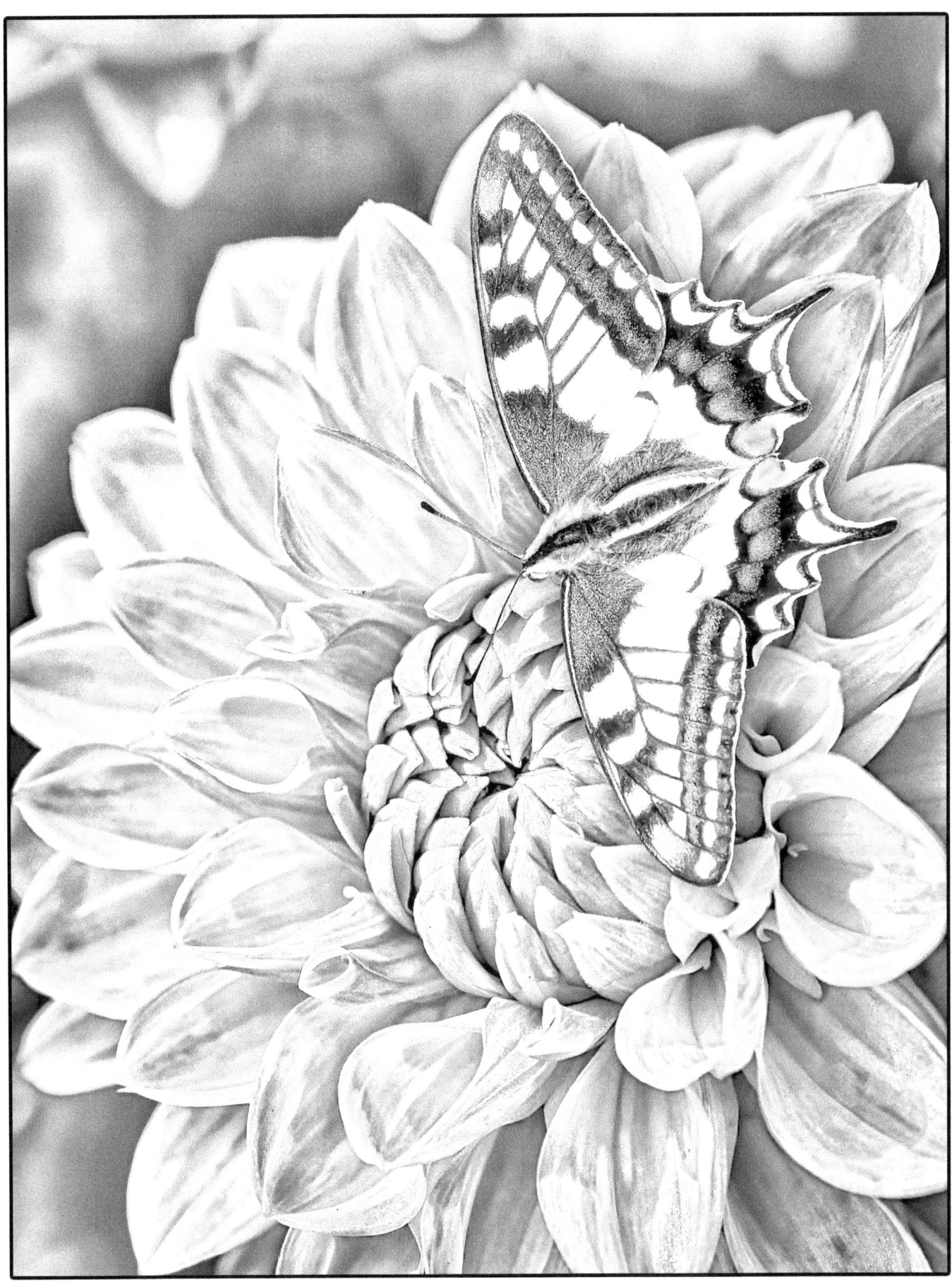

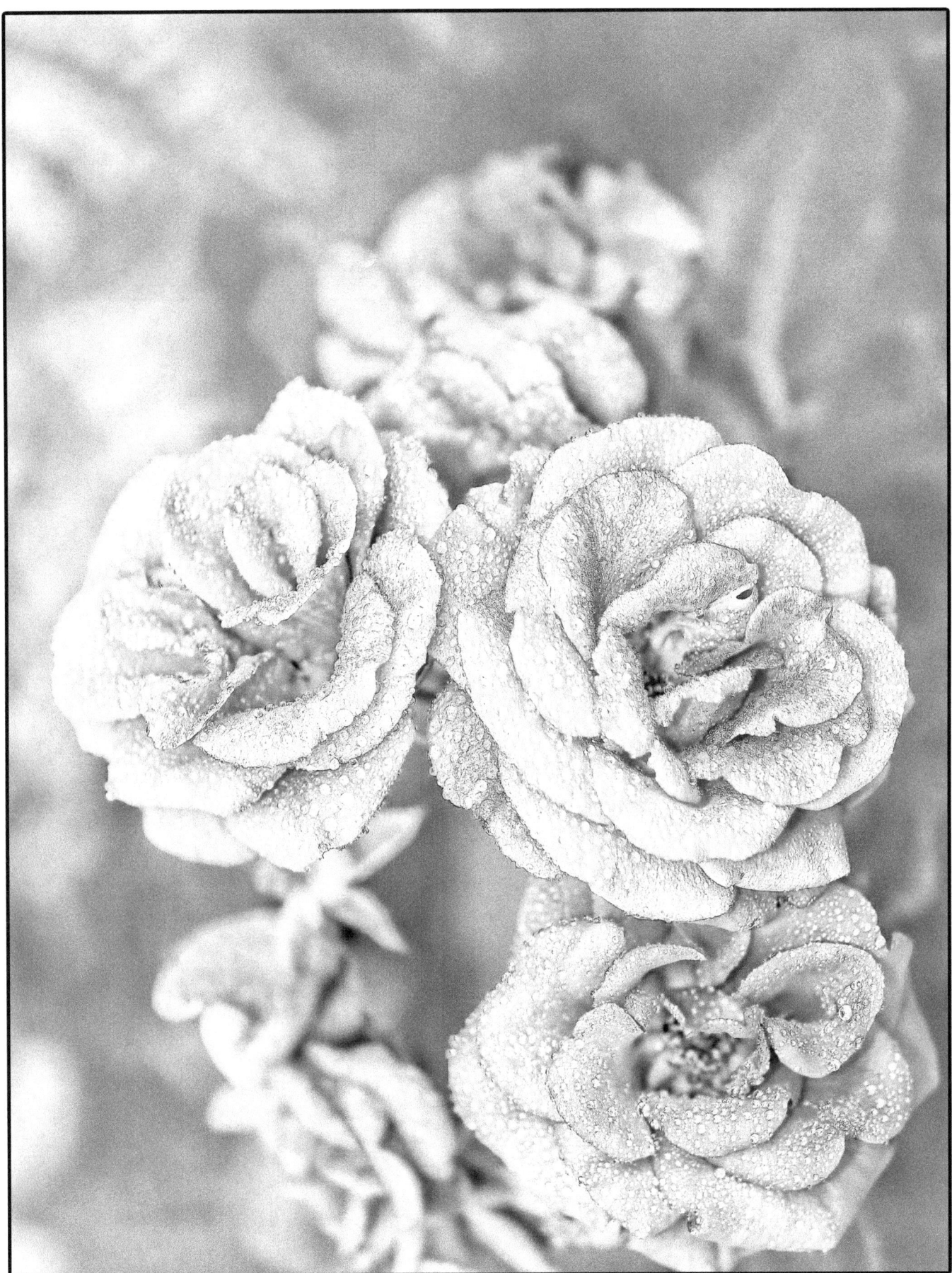

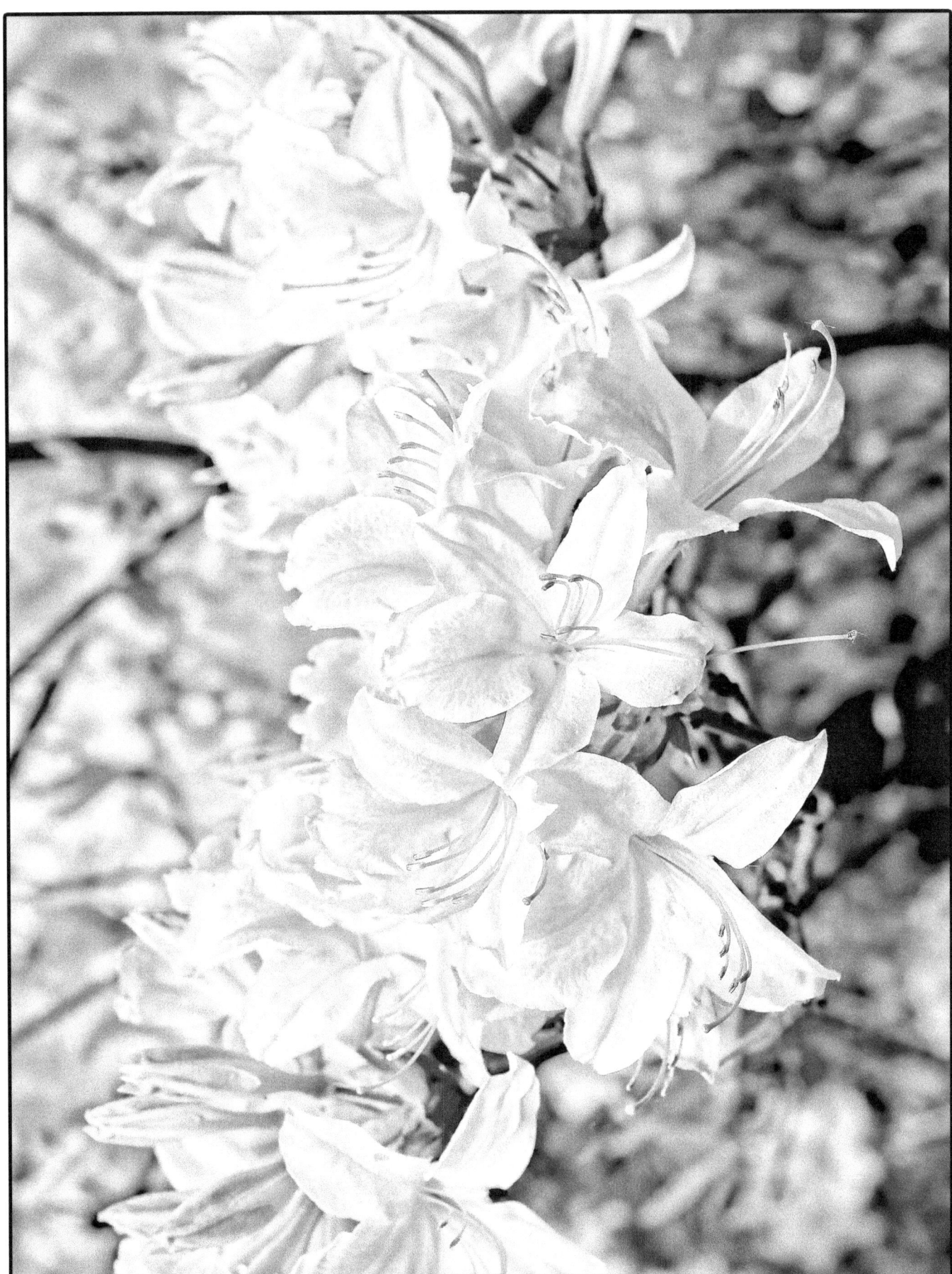

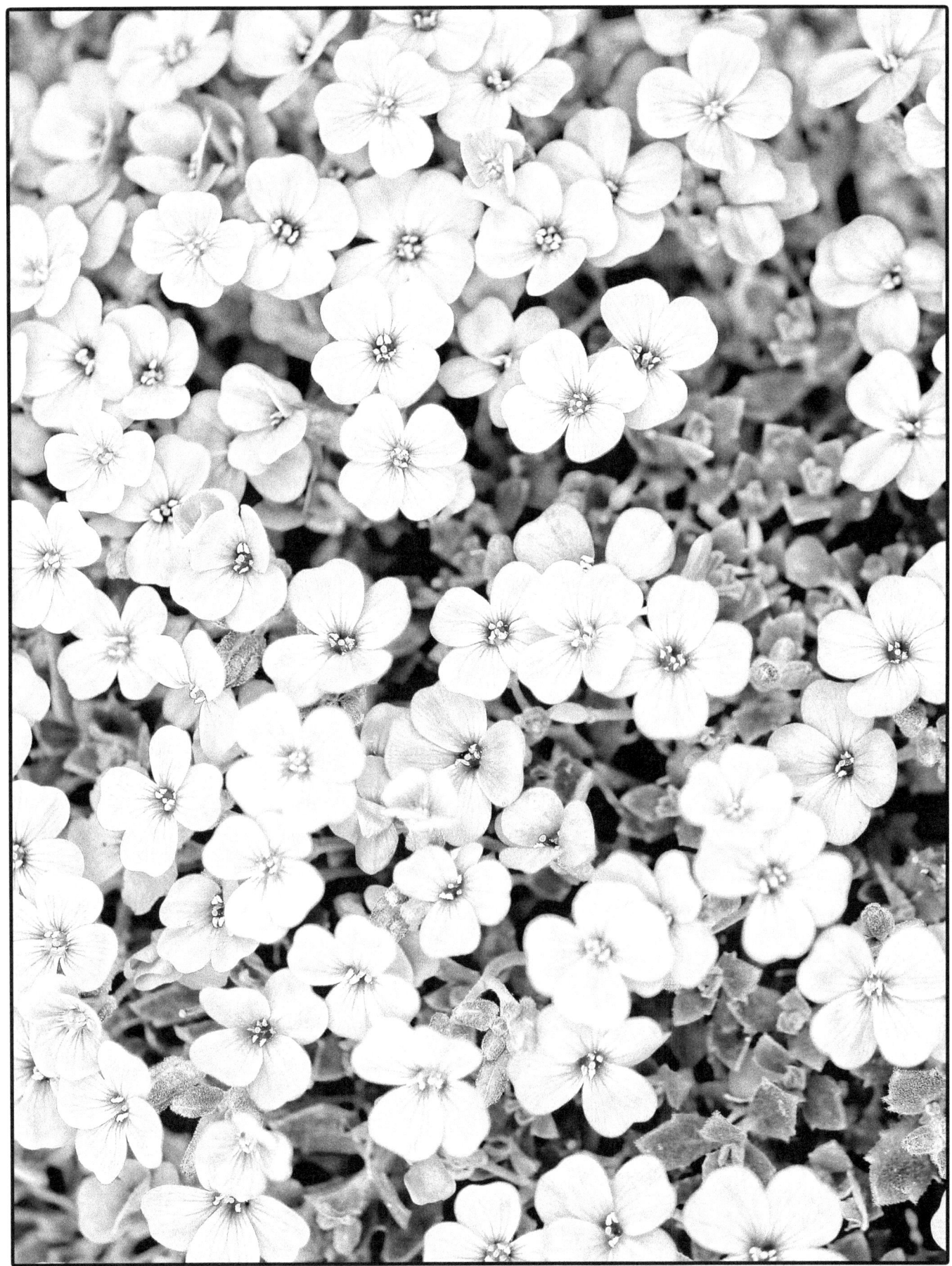

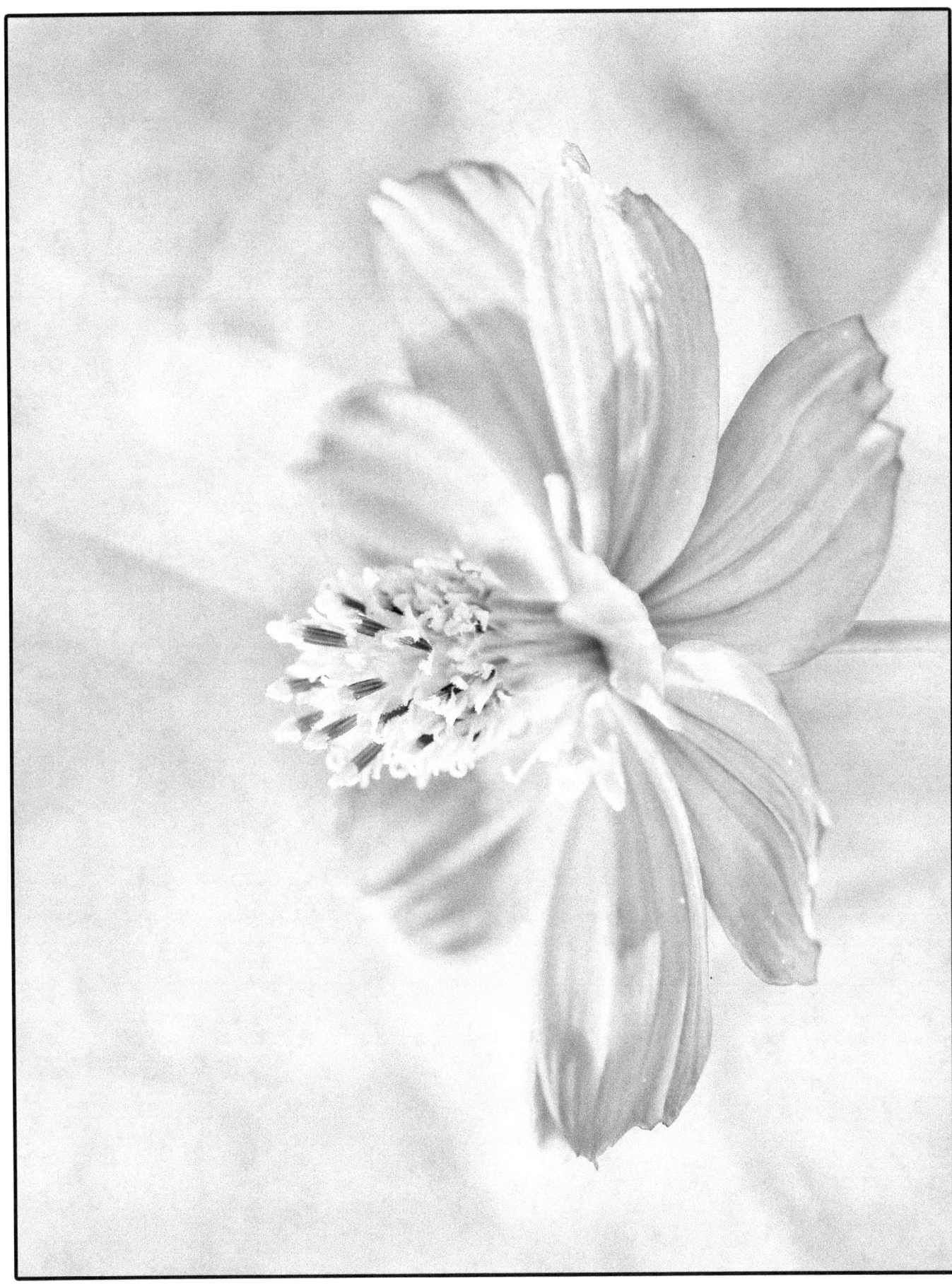

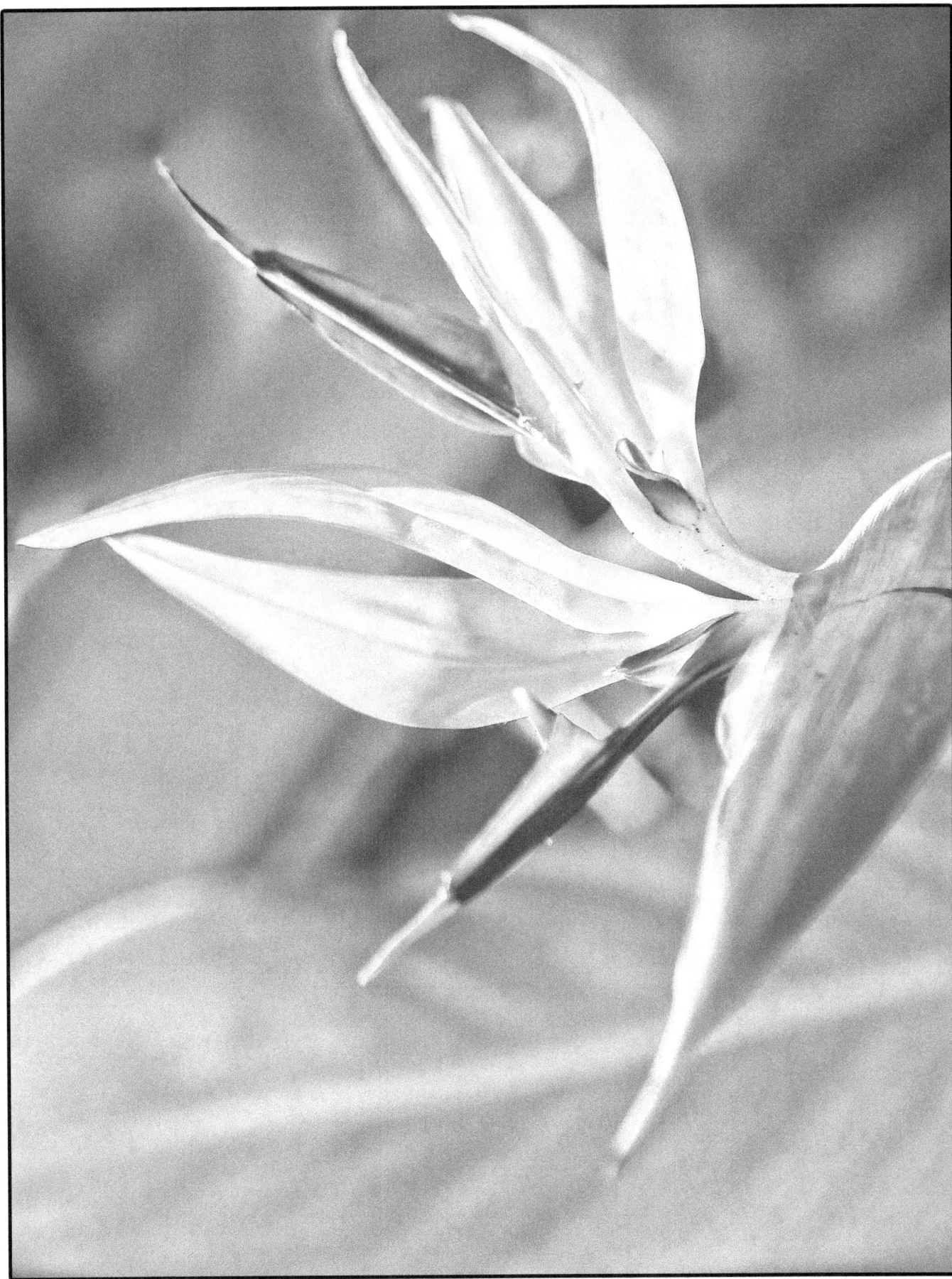

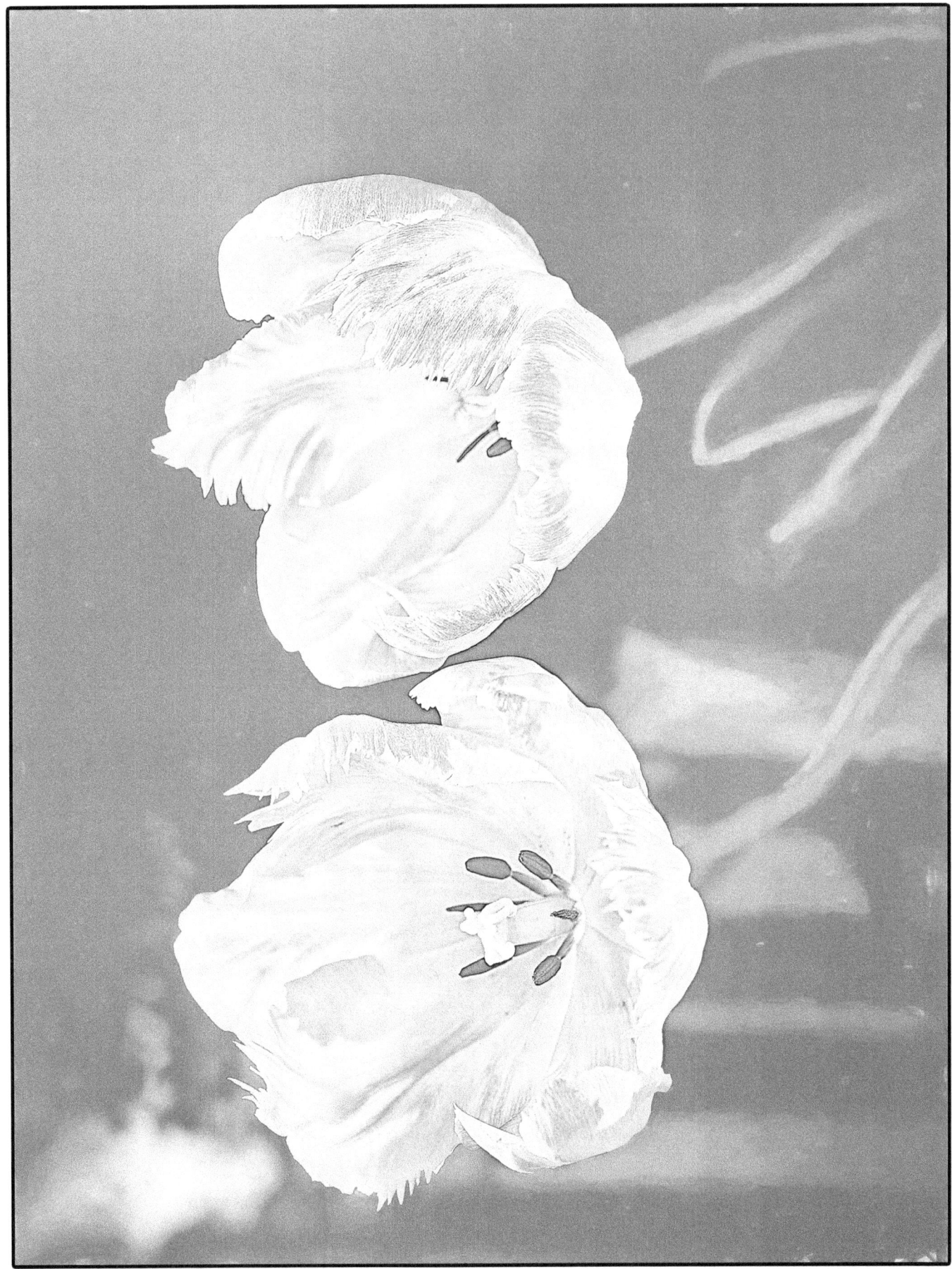

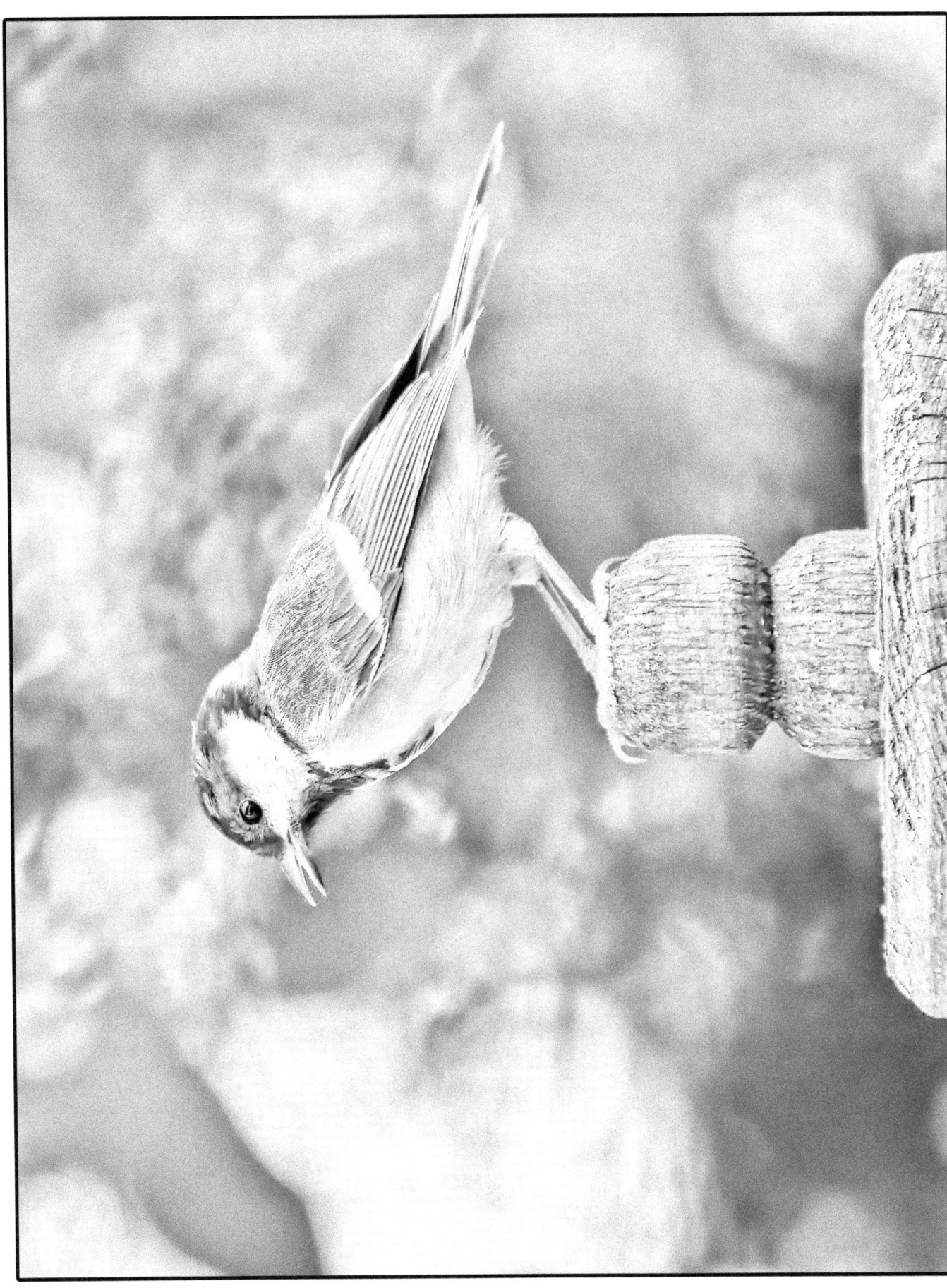

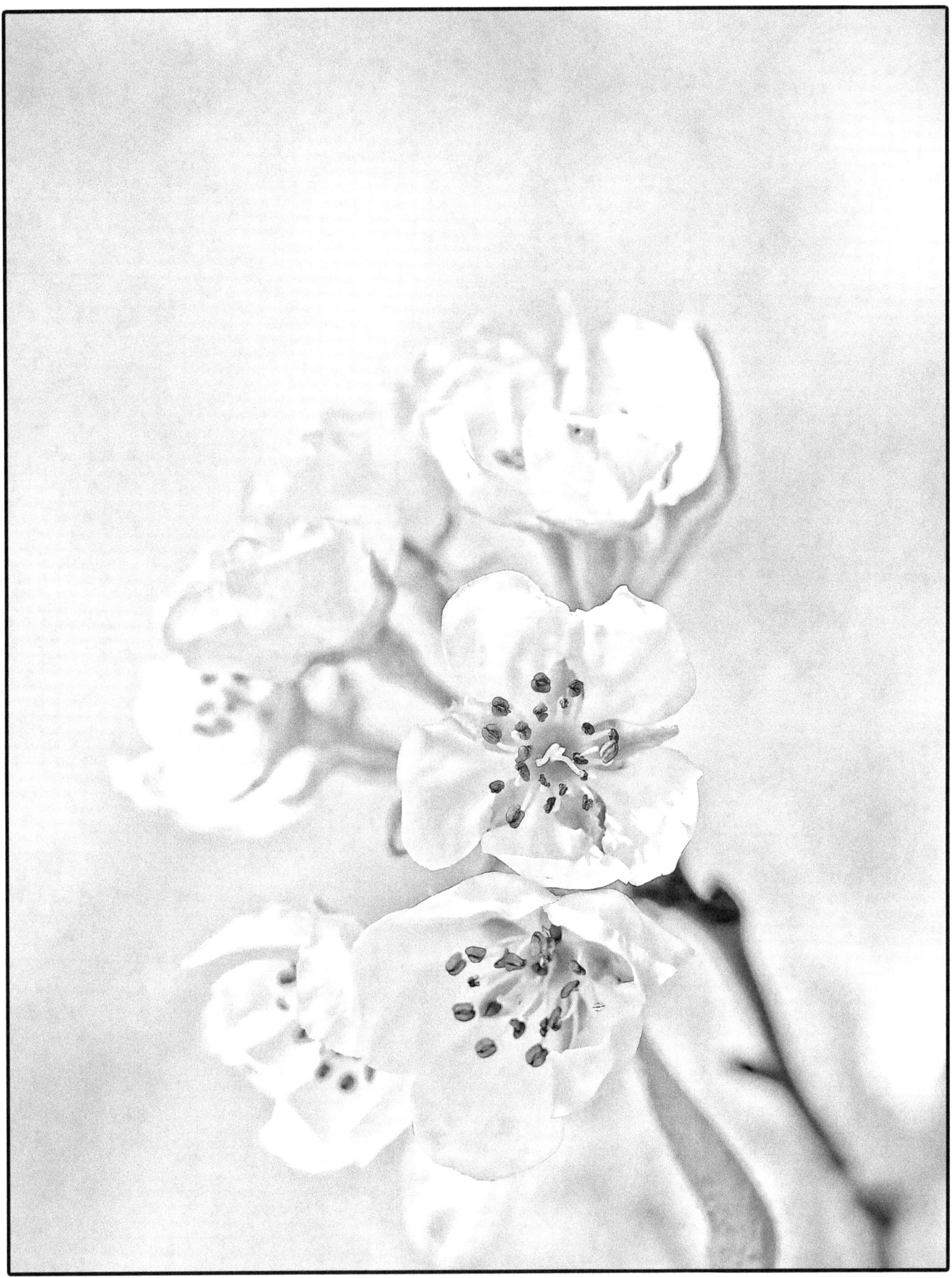

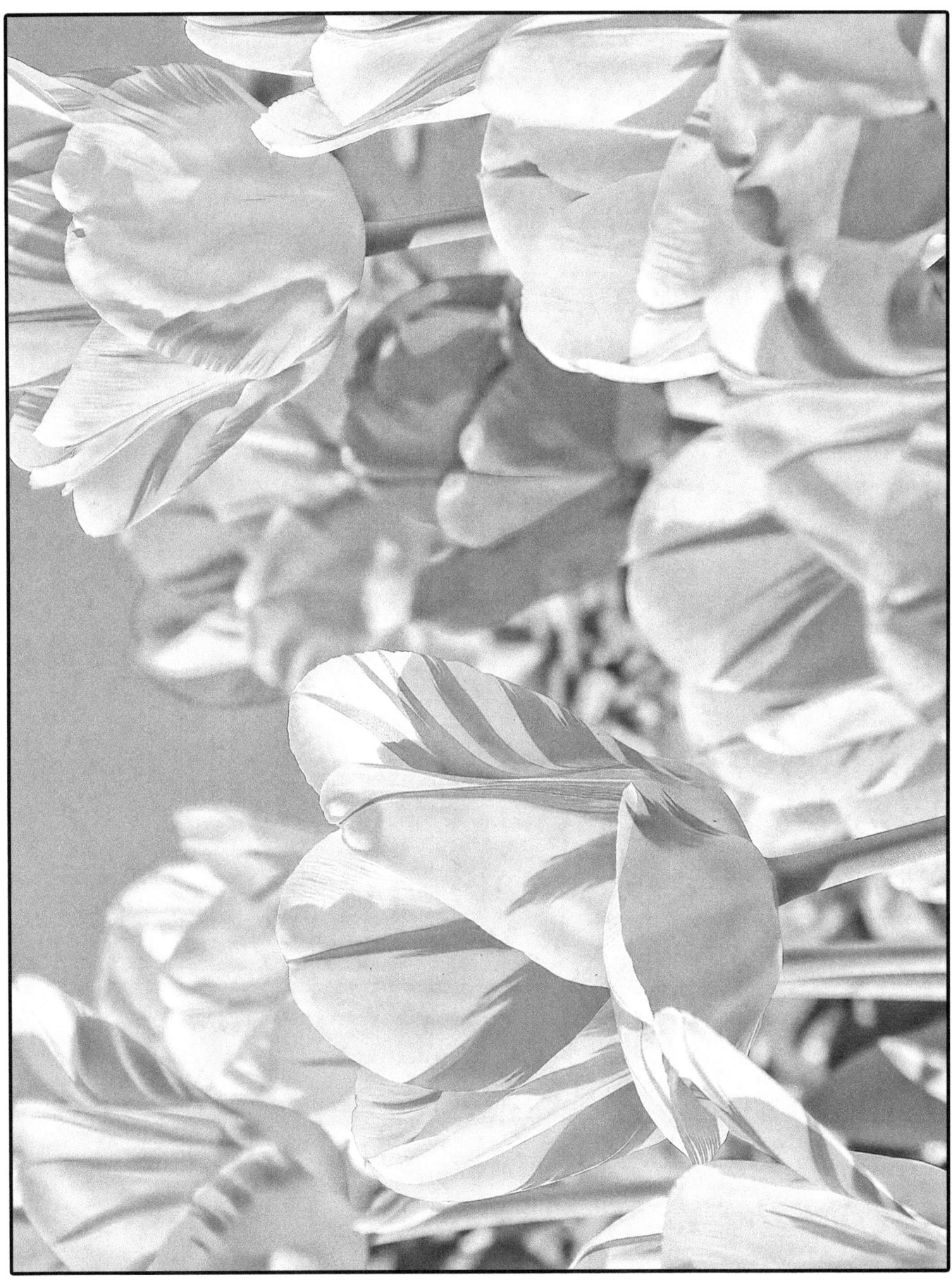

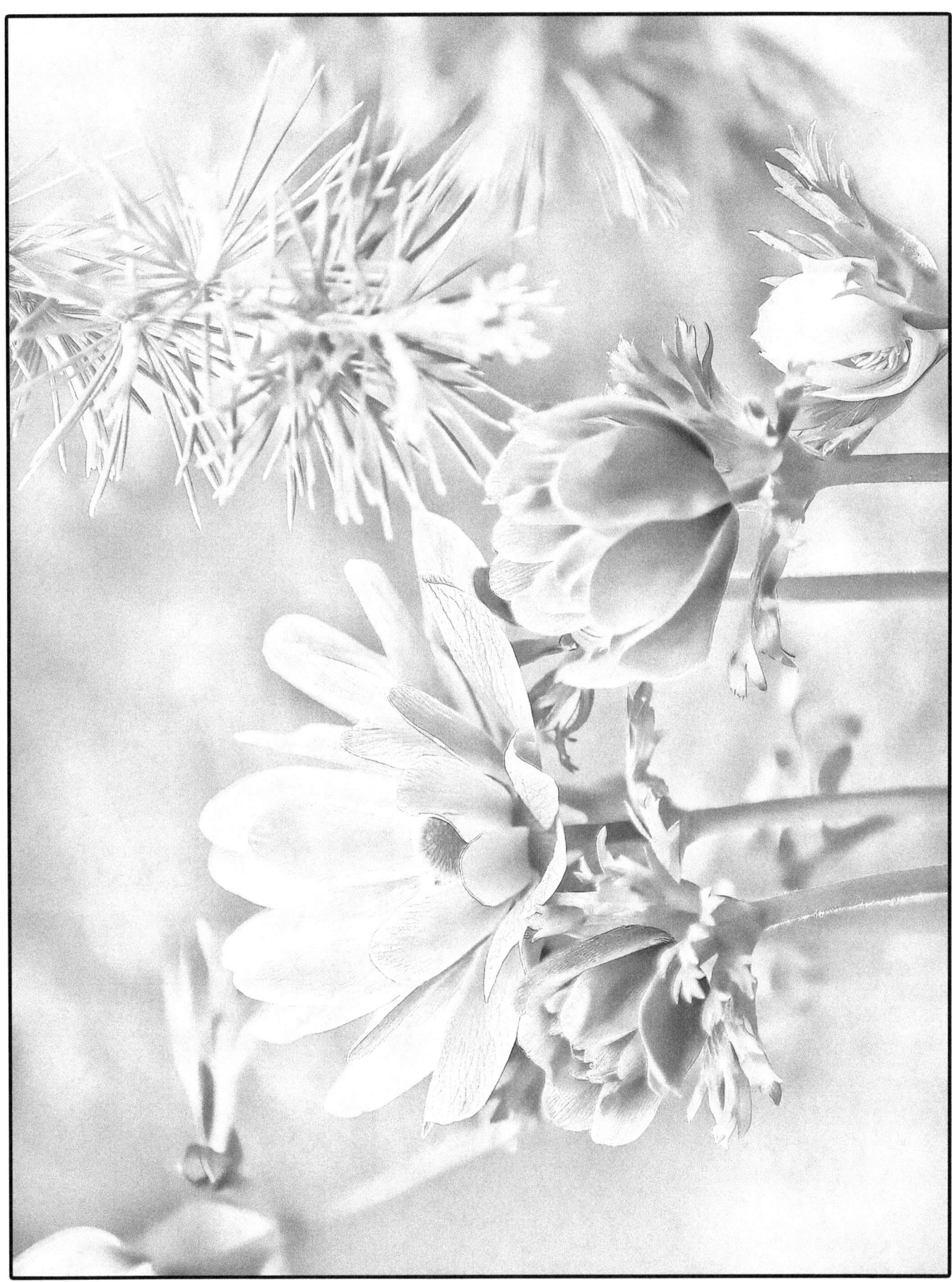

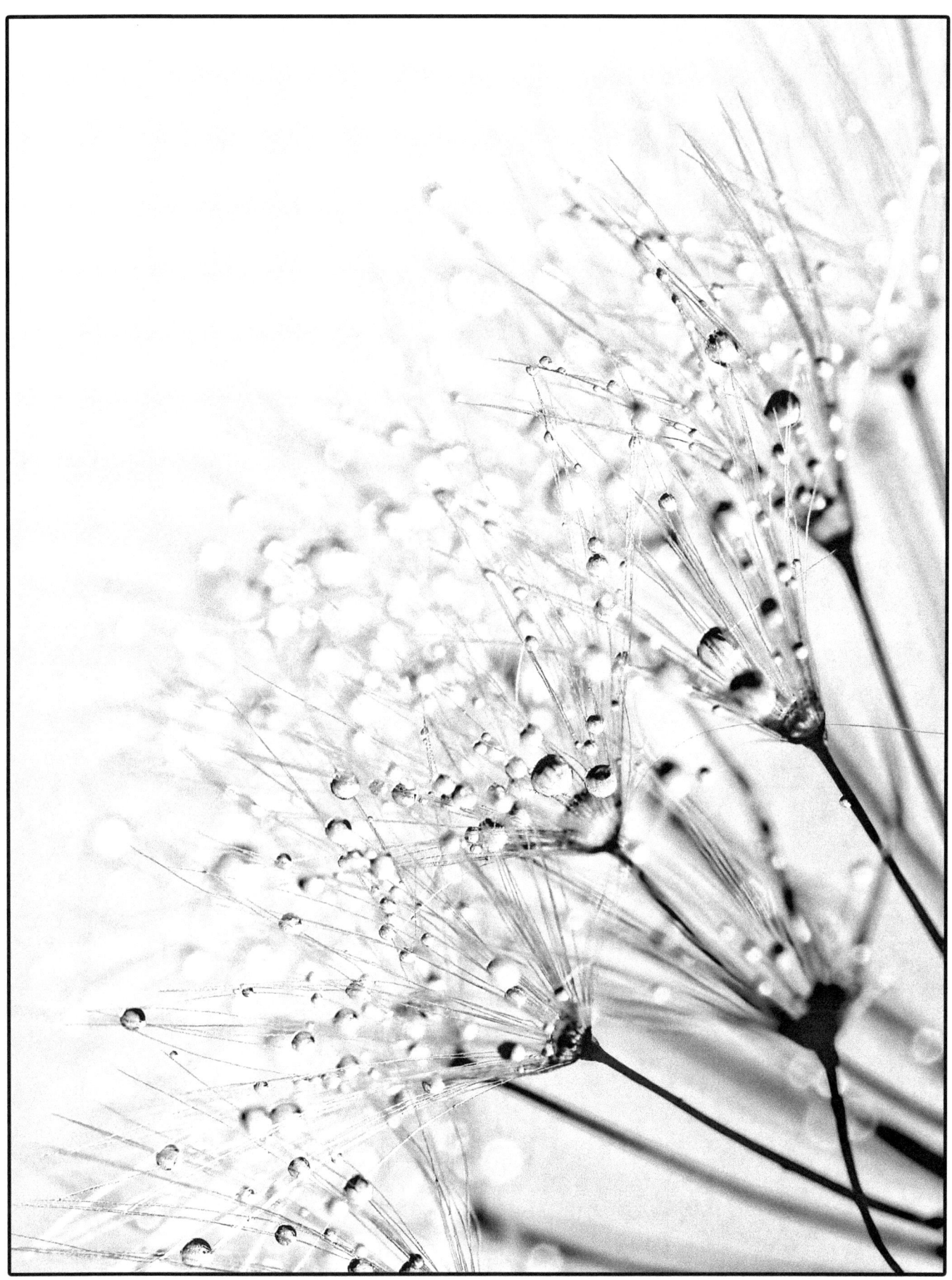

Mini Guide - cutting

1. Optionally: before coloring or painting you can cut all pages out using a long ruler and a craft knife (snap off knife, paper utility knife).

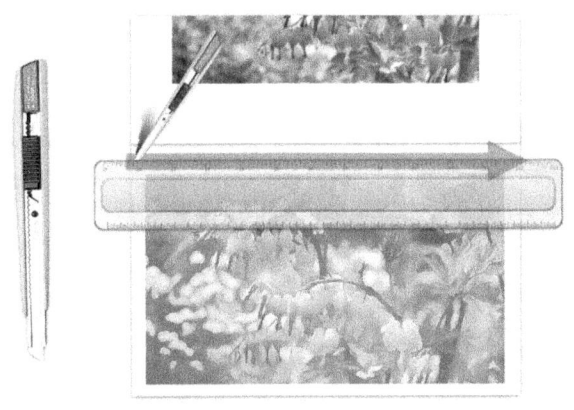
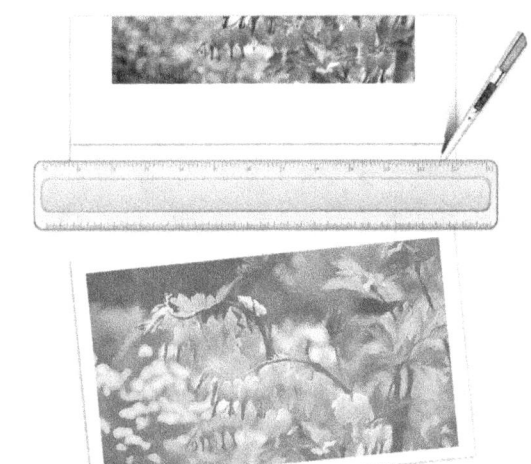

Then place the page on a large sheet of paper or plastic.

2. If the paper curls you can use **paperweights** or **magnets** (in this case you need a metal plate under the picture). Or you can choose a better solution: **"Kenting Magnetic Pad K4M"**

This way you will have more space, and painting will be more comfortable.

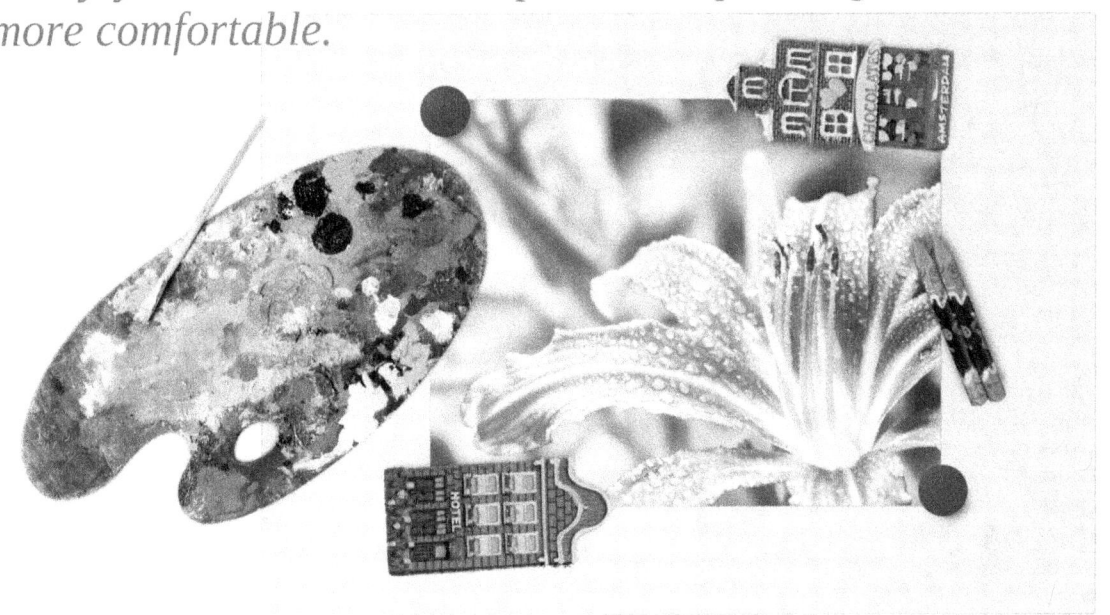

About Coloring and Painting

*You'll get the best artistic results, painting like, using a **hybrid coloring** method:*

1) The first way
- color the fragments with colored pencils
- then use acrylic paints to make the colors more vivid and saturated.

Always allow the paint to dry before applying the next layer.

2) Or the second way
- start with markers
- then finish with Pebbles Chalks (for the background)
A very lovely effect.

*About markers. They might bleed through the page, but images are printed on one side. Use a thick cardboard or bristol and put it under your drawing (**if you don't want to cut pages from the book**).*

*Try also some neon colors and markers. **Pastel pencils** are also a good choice.*

*Another way: use acrylics only (**acrylics are better than watercolors for this coloring book**), but don't use too much water. This paper doesn't like water. And add some gold and silver paints.*

☺ Just try different media and enjoy! Soon you will gain the experience.

Did you know ...

About dark and gray images.

- Every picture can be beautifully colored, even when it is dark or gray (A). How? You can use two methods:

- Apply dark pastel pencils (better) or colored pencils. This will increase the contrast of the image (B).
or
- Cover the gray with bright, opaque acrylic paints (C).

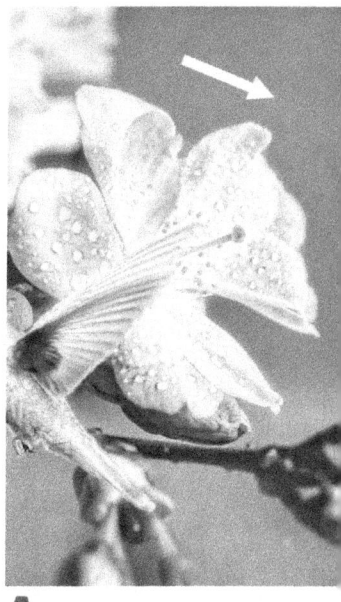

A

Opaque acrylic paints are best suited for dark images. If you can paint, good work and nice colors will come out because the paint will cover the "ugly", dark print.

- Pastels in the form of pencils also cover well. **Pastel pencils** are better than classic pastels because you can paint small details.

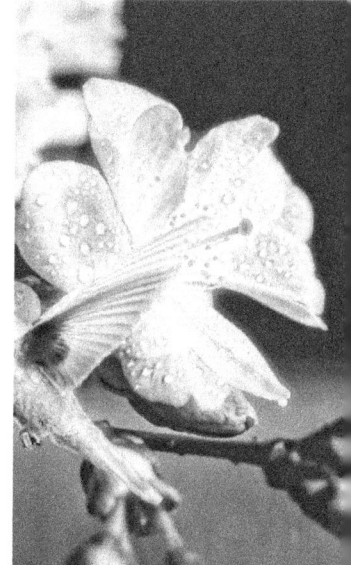

B

- Acrylic paints give similar effects to oil paints, but are as cheap and easy to use as watercolors. Watercolors are not suitable for this paper and are too transparent, and oil paints require more skills. Meanwhile, acrylic paints combine the advantages of both types, here's the reason why I like them. **There are transparent and opaque acrylic paints**. There are also special gels (e.g: "Gelex") that can brighten colors and make them more opaque.

- For these reasons, **do not dilute acrylic paints with water or use less water**. You can mix paints, but rather do not dilute them. If you need a light color, simply mix dark paint with white or yellow.

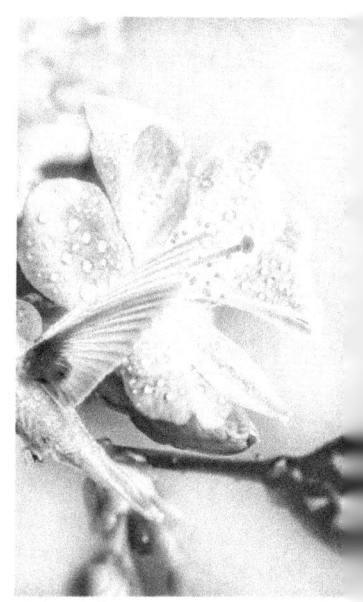

C

How do you make colors deep, vivid and saturated, just like on the screen?

Colored pencils give a nice effect, but sometimes the picture may be pale, not like my works.

The best effects are created using **hybrid coloring** *and a large number of layers: use black fineliner to draw outlines. Then apply the markers. Next some colored pencils. Also white pencil. Finally, acrylic paints. This method creates beautiful colors and contrast.*

At this point it is no longer ordinary, amateur coloring, but real art. The effect will be like a painting. See examples on the cover and more on my Amazon page. Soon I will post images on Twitter and YouTube. Soon I will also publish a larger coloring guide and several books in color called **"Coloring Like Painting"**.

People are often surprised that "their coloring" does not give such beautiful effects as on examples.

There are two reasons. The computer screen gives different colors than printing or colored pencils. Secondly, the poor effects result from a lack of experience in using painting techniques and tools.

Search YouTube for grayscale coloring videos. The best colored works look better than the original color photos! And they are simply beautiful and romantic. They have a mood, and the authors paint on them things that were not in the gray photo: flowers, elves, rays of light ...

At the End

This is my private email, so you can ask me anything you want:
lech.balcerzak.books@gmail.com

Or if you prefer Twitter:
https://twitter.com/LeshekAboutLife

Have a nice day,
Lech

PS
Remember the gold rule: the result does not depend on whether you buy expensive colored pencils and paints. This is a common mistake. The most expensive painting tools from well-known companies will not automatically give you a good effect.

It does not depend on expensive colored pencils or the quality of paper. The effect depends more on your experience. So color, paint and practice. Apply more layers. You will gain practice with time.

www.ingramcontent.com/pod-product-compliance
Lightning Source LLC
Chambersburg PA
CBHW062335220526

45469CB00008B/2720